Encountering
Jesus

Encountering Jesus

How People Come to Faith and Discover Discipleship

Anthony J. Gittins

WIPF & STOCK · Eugene, Oregon

Wipf and Stock Publishers
199 W 8th Ave, Suite 3
Eugene, OR 97401

Encountering Jesus
How People Come to Faith and Discover Discipleship
By Gittins, Anthony J., CSPS
Copyright©2002 by Gittins, Anthony J., CSPS
ISBN 13: 978-1-5326-4252-4
Publication date 10/17/2017
Previously published by Liguori/Triumph, 2002

In memory of
Damian Lundy, F.S.C.
(1944–1996),
brother, teacher,
musician, poet, artist,
friend to many,
gentle man of God,
proclaimer of Good News.

Contents

Preface

Perhaps twenty years ago I had the great pleasure and privilege of working with Damian Lundy, F.S.C., on a short retreat for young people in England. Damian, a De la Salle Brother, was a large, charming person and a wonderful storyteller. He held a restive teenage audience spellbound when he told the story of the man born blind (see chapter 9 of John's Gospel).

Damian's retelling was a fine blend of biblical scholarship lightly worn, imagination consciously developed, and the storyteller's art graciously given by God. I remember being impressed by this way of proclaiming the Good News, noticing how attractive it was to young people, and becoming conscious of its power to deepen faith in Jesus. The ministry, the homiletic skills, and the touch of the showman in Damian Lundy were gifts to many.

About a decade later, I was invited to give a retreat to the Franciscan Missionaries of Mary (F.M.M.) in Providence, Rhode Island. Partly because the Sisters came from several different cultural backgrounds and had lived widely varying experiences, and partly because they were of what is called "the senior cohort" and retired from earlier and more active ministries, I chose to focus the retreat around encounters between Jesus and various women and men, insiders and outsiders, people of substance and people regarded as sinners. The theme was "Coming to Faith Through Encounters With Jesus." The retreat was well received, most of the conferences were videotaped, and Sisters who had not been present—and some who had—were able to review the talks at leisure.

In the jubilee year, 2000, I offered a similar retreat to the Sisters of

St. Joseph (C.S.J.) of Wichita, Kansas, choosing as a theme, "Encountering Jesus," and essentially covering the same ground as in Rhode Island. But on this occasion the response was such that I felt these stories might translate into a short book. A significant number of comments indicated these women found the accounts to be not only interesting and somewhat novel in the context of a retreat, but actually formative for them. The fact that this approach to the New Testament "made Jesus come alive" was most encouraging. Before the retreat was over, I determined to turn these "encounters" into prose, and told this to the group in attendance.

In 2001, a retreat for the Sisters of St. Joseph (C.S.J.), of Baden, Pennsylvania, included some further reflections on encounters with Jesus: this time specifically and only between Jesus and women. During the course of that retreat, I began to write down the narratives of some of the encounters found in the following pages.

It is important for me to record my gratitude to the three communities which offered me the opportunity to pursue particular trains of thought, and to acknowledge that if they had not so graciously accepted the ideas expressed, I certainly would not have attempted to accumulate and elaborate these stories.

One of the main reasons for this retelling is that it might more explicitly identify and emphasize the way people come to faith and discover discipleship. Typically, the stories demonstrate that there are often a number of stages, or steps, involved. The easiest way to identify these steps is simply to note exactly what each person says, and the sequence in which they say it, during their encounter with Jesus. Apart from the rare exception when someone immediately identifies Jesus as God—in other words, makes an explicit faith statement—most people's journey to faith is a little slower. Some identify him first by name, others simply by addressing him as "sir." But as we watch how the story unfolds, we should also notice how their faith develops. Readers may look for a three-step or a four-step approach to faith, as a person moves to an ever more specific identification of Jesus as the person in whom they put their faith. This is an interesting, enlightening, and sometimes surprising exercise.

The work of writing up each of the following encounters took place in airports and hotel rooms from Perth to New York and from Thailand to England. For example, the story of Zacchaeus was begun in Tokyo and completed in Singapore, that of the bent-over woman was written between Pennsylvania and Pakistan, and the list could go on. A draft of the entire book was completed in Manila, Philippines, where I had the good fortune to be teaching early in 2002.

These particular stories have been chosen because they provide a certain amount of detail that can be grist for meditation. Other favorite New Testament stories, those which are either too short or not primarily concerned with a coming to faith or discovering discipleship, are not included. I have tried to follow the sequence of stories as presented in Mark's Gospel. Where stories appear in more than one form, I have most often chosen Mark's account, both because it is probably the earliest we have and also because Mark is such a consummate storyteller. However, I chose Matthew's account for the stories of the walking on the water and the Canaanite woman because certain significant details are included that help to illustrate the theme of coming to faith. Likewise, there are several stories that only Luke gives us, and two (the woman at the well and the man born blind) that only occur in John. Whenever I have not used Mark's account, I have tried to insert the story into the overall scheme of Mark's Gospel for the sake of coherence. But this has not always been possible, especially in the case of the post-Resurrection stories.

Unless otherwise indicated, I have used the New Revised Standard Version (NRSV) of the New Testament. On several occasions, however, I also refer to the Jerusalem Bible's (JB) translation. Because the most accessible parallel text version uses the Revised Standard Version (RSV),[1] I have occasionally chosen to use that as well. For copyright reasons, I have not changed the scriptural text in order to make the language inclusive. But when not directly quoting the text, I did use inclusive language.

This modest and unscholarly book is dedicated to the memory of Brother Damian Lundy, a man of faith, humor, and courage, and also to those religious women who encouraged me to pursue this particular method of faith formation. This book is also a reminder that time is short, delays are long, and that there is something to be said for laptops at airports after all.

Manila, Philippines

February 16, 2002

Endnotes

1. *Gospel Parallels: A Synopsis of the First Three Gospels.* Burton H. Throckmorton, Jr. (ed), Camden, N.J.: T. Nelson: 1967 [1949].

CHAPTER ONE

From Paralysis to Praise

(Mk 2:1–12)[2]

(1) *When he [Jesus] returned to Capernaum after some days, it was reported that he was at home.* (2) *So many gathered around that there was no longer room for them, not even in front of the door; and he was speaking the word to them.* (3) *Then some people came, bringing to him a paralyzed man, carried by four of them.* (4) *And when they could not bring him to Jesus because of the crowd, they removed the roof above him; and after having dug through it, they let down the mat on which the paralytic lay.* (5) *When Jesus saw their faith, he said to the paralytic, "Son, your sins are forgiven."* (6) *Now some of the scribes were sitting there, questioning in their hearts,* (7) *"Why does this fellow speak in this way? It is blasphemy! Who can forgive sins but God alone?"* (8) *At once Jesus perceived in his spirit that they were discussing these questions among themselves; and he said to them, "Why do you raise such questions in your hearts?* (9) *Which is easier, to say to the paralytic, 'Your sins are forgiven,' or to say, 'Stand up and take your mat and walk'?* (10) *But so that you may know that the Son of Man has authority on earth to forgive sins"—he said to the paralytic—* (11) *"I say to you, stand up, take your mat and go to your home."* (12) *And he stood up, and immediately took the mat and went out before all of them; so that they were all amazed and glorified God, saying, "We have never seen anything like this!"*

A t the very outset of his ministry, Jesus declared his hand: "The time is fulfilled, and the Kingdom of God has come near; repent, and believe in the good news" (Mk 1:15). Shortly afterwards, having called the first four disciples, Jesus found that he needed to clarify his purpose. He would need to do this several times over the following months and, at times, his exasperation would show. On this occasion, Peter, excited that Jesus had cured his mother-in-law, seems to want to act like an entrepreneur or impresario: in contemporary language, he wants to become Jesus' agent. He hints that a partnership between Jesus and himself could make a thriving business. But Jesus will have none of it. Very clearly he says to Peter, "Let us go on to the neighboring towns, so that I may proclaim the message there also; for that is what I came out to do." The text continues, "And he went throughout Galilee, proclaiming the message in their synagogues and casting out demons" (Mk 1:38–39).

After curing Peter's mother-in-law, Jesus' first recorded "work of power" (miracle) concerns a lone leper. The details are few, but this encounter sets the stage. At the end of that account Jesus is already becoming lionized and is unable to pass unrecognized. After some days spent attending to the people in the countryside, he returns to his base at Capernaum. But the news is soon out.

Our first story will show, among other things, the importance of community, both for getting things done and for nurturing faith. Jesus finds himself mobbed by an excited and sympathetic crowd that has gathered to listen to him. Some people had come not simply to hear his words, but to seek healing. There were four such people on this particular day carrying a paralyzed man on a litter (or mat). The paralyzed man could do little to help himself, and in fact, he depended almost entirely on other people. Less fervent friends might have bowed to the impossible: there was simply no way they could get close to Jesus in this large a crowd, no way to catch his eye or make themselves heard. But these are not just fair-weather friends, they are more than simply determined: they are *driven*. How else can we explain their extraordinary purposefulness, resourcefulness, and even recklessness? Their purpose is clear: to get to Jesus, come what may. Their resourcefulness is unquestionable: they will climb to the flat roof, remove thatch and branches, and even the tiles. Their recklessness may be more like a calculated risk: perhaps they knew the owner and would promise to make restitution for whatever mess they made; perhaps they would be able to appeal to the community for understanding and accept-ance of their emergency. Nevertheless, they seem to have acted single-mindedly, very promptly, and with remarkable conviction.

So they contrived a dramatic entrance. By the time they had swung the mat and its occupant into the room, Jesus was certainly aware of them. How could he not be? There must have been quite a commo-tion as they came through the roof. And there would have been dust—perhaps choking, blinding dust—as they landed in the midst of eve-ryone and before Jesus. And how does he respond? Does he object to the interruption or criticize the imprudence or destructiveness of their *modus operandi*? Does he see them as wrongheaded simpletons, or worse? Does he, perhaps, admire their initiative?

Jesus does none of these things. He does not appear to be think-ing along these lines at all. All we are told, very simply and directly, is that, "When Jesus saw their faith, he said to the paralytic, 'Son, your sins are forgiven'" (v. 5). This is an astounding response. It represents an instant, yet penetrating, diagnosis. It demonstrates knowledge, clar-ity of purpose, and personal authority. It confirms how attentive[3] and responsive Jesus is. And yet his diagnosis appears quite unrelated to the paralysis, and his response is obviously not a work of power or miraculous cure at all, but a declaration of divine forgiveness. What are we to make of this?

"Some of the scribes" (v. 6) immediately respond like a Greek cho-rus. They ask (rhetorically) who Jesus thinks he is and how he could possibly speak in this way. But, curiously, they do not seem to make any connection between the physical condition of the paralytic and Jesus' response. Those who read or hear this story will be aware that Jesus "saw [the] faith" of the group of men. But the scribes are not privy to this information, and they simply see and hear Jesus' response, which seems to make no sense under these circumstances. They are not really watching what Jesus is doing or trying to understand his pedagogy in this context. They are simply looking for trouble, looking for something to criticize. The scribes of this story are ill-disposed, antagonistic, and acting in bad faith. And Jesus can read them like a book.

The good faith of the paralytic and his supporters stands in dramatic contrast to the bad faith of the scribes, and Jesus will confound the latter even as he affirms the former. He will also drive home a lesson, very powerfully and impressively, to the scribes, and this lesson will not be lost on the crowd either. More than this, Jesus will publicly shame the scribes, which could prove to be a very dangerous move.

Jesus, then, has already identified the faith that characterizes the little group of men, one sick and the others his helpers. This will always be his primary intention: to look for faith, to engender faith, to support faith, and to reward faith when he finds it. In this case, no word of faith has been spoken, but Jesus has already attributed faith to all five of the men. He saw *their* faith. Later he would be more explicit about the dimensions of faith. Faith is a steadfast commitment to God, despite appearances, and without proof. Faith bespeaks a relationship with God; it is not simply religious knowledge. It is not those who say "Lord, Lord," who demonstrate faith and are eligible for the Kingdom, but those who do God's will (see Mt 7:21). And in these men, Jesus can see some encouraging traces of faith. Probably unlettered and unsophisticated, they have clung to God's promises and continue to believe in God's own faithfulness. From where did their faith come? We simply do not know.

Scholars speak of agonistic cultures, societies in which life is perceived as a contest. Those who want to count for something must engage in tests of strength: not always tests of physical strength, and indeed not always very mature or serious tests. In the present case, the scribes have become caught up in an agonistic mood: they want a demonstration that Jesus' words ("your sins are forgiven") are not simply idle utterings. Jesus, for his part, has no need to respond to such petty challenges and will tell his followers that this is not the way for disciples to gain stature before God. But in any culture, one must, at times, use fire to combat fire, and Jesus is not entirely averse to a contest, especially one through which he can show the works of God. So Jesus responds.

"Which is easier, to say 'your sins are forgiven,' or to say, 'stand up and take your mat and walk' "? (v. 9), inquires Jesus, rhetorically and not so innocently. It is a trap. They cannot avoid it. It is not even necessary that he humiliate them by forcing an answer. Everyone knows that talk is cheaper than action. Everyone also knows that it is much easier to *say* "Your sins are forgiven." If Jesus can *do* what is more difficult, he will thereby demonstrate that he has the power to accomplish what, by their own admission, is apparently easier: to forgive sins. The more we think about it, the more we see the trap and the impossibility of escape. Yet Jesus only indirectly demonstrates his authority over sin. Even if the people actually see that he has accomplished what they believe to be more difficult, they will not see sins being forgiven. That kind of sight—insight or perception—requires a capacity for making logical connections, plus good faith, complemented by trust in the one who demonstrates the power to heal a paralytic.

Turning now to the paralytic (who has not said a word), Jesus prepares to perform a work of power, a miraculous healing. But before he does, he reiterates that his action is primarily a sign, something that points to something else. It is not simply a healing that Jesus is interested in, but demonstrating "that the Son of Man has authority on earth to forgive sins" (v. 10). In other words, he is claiming to act in a godly way, in fact, in a way that only God can act. That is the purpose for his miracles, and faith is the trigger that releases this power. Since he has already identified the faith in the sick man *and his friends*, Jesus will now reward that faith and allow the people to catch a glimpse of God's wonderful works.

Still without a word, not even a word of gratitude, but already endorsed by Jesus as a man of faith, the paralytic immediately stands straight and tall. Such is the power of the healing[4] word, it instantaneously accomplishes what it says. The man, now healed, picks up his mat and walks through the crowd that opens up to make way for him. Of his companions we hear nothing more, but we are left to wonder: how will the faith that brought them this far continue to affect their

future lives and those of the greater community? With respect to the
immediate community however, we are left with no doubts: "They
were all amazed and glorified God, saying, 'We have never seen anything like this'" (v. 12). They were *all* amazed. Yet not everyone glorified God: the scribes, losers in this competition, had lost face and failed
to come to faith. But they would live to fight another day.

This turn of events leaves us with one small thought to ponder:
"Jesus saw their faith" (v. 5). If this is the case, then faith can charac-
terize a whole community.[5] It is not simply a private or individual
matter. This insight can be particularly helpful when we feel depleted
or burdened. Sometimes we may feel depleted, our faith in tatters,
threadbare. In such cases, blessed are we if we have a community to
love and pray for us. Even when our faith seems so very fragile, we
may be sustained by the faith of those around us. At other times we
may feel quite overburdened and incapable of generating any further
response. In such cases, blessed are we if we are supported and raised
up by the helping hands of others.

But there may not be times when our faith seems as strong as the
mustard seed, and when God is palpably present in our lives. At these
times, not only will more be demanded of us, but we will be expected
to turn to and raise up our suffering brothers and sisters. In this story,
we see a man who is weak, but sustained and, literally, carried by strong
friends. We see friends joining together, each picking up a corner of
his mattress, knowing that none could carry it alone, but together, as
a team, they could transport their paralyzed friend to a place of healing.

Our Christian commitment is measured not only by our strength
but by our collaboration, and not by our weakness but by our willingness to be raised up and supported by the community. "And Jesus saw
their faith." May this be true of us, as it was of them.

Endnotes

2. See also Matthew 9:1–8; and Luke 5:17–26.
3. The Greek word *therapeuein*, which gives us the word "thera-

peutic" in English, is most commonly translated as "to heal." Its first meaning, however, is "to be attentive," in the sense of to attend to someone's needs.

4. There is a useful distinction to be made, between (physical) curing and (spiritual) healing. See the story of the ten lepers (Ch. 9, below).

5. See Bernard Lonergan, *Method in Theology*, 1972: 130–1, and page 51 below.

CHAPTER TWO

A Man Possessed

(Mk 5:1–20)

(1) *They came to the other side of the sea, to the country of the Gerasenes.* (2) *And when he had stepped out of the boat, immediately a man out of the tombs with an unclean spirit met him.* (3) *He lived among the tombs; and no one could restrain him any more, even with a chain;* (4) *for he had often been restrained with shackles and chains, but the chains he wrenched apart, and shackles he broke in pieces; and no one had the strength to subdue him.* (5) *Night and day among the tombs and on the mountains he was always howling and bruising himself with stones.* (6) *When he saw Jesus from a distance, he ran and bowed down before him;* (7) *and he shouted at the top of his voice, "What have you to do with me, Jesus, Son of the Most High God? I adjure you by God, do not torment me."* (8) *For he had said to him, "Come out of the man, you unclean spirit!"* (9) *Then Jesus asked him, "What is your name?" He replied, "My name is Legion; for we are many."* (10) *He begged him earnestly not to send them out of the country.* (11) *Now there on the hillside a great herd of swine was feeding;* (12) *and the unclean spirits begged him, "Send us into the swine; let us enter them."* (13) *So he gave them permission. And the unclean spirits came out and entered the swine; and the herd, numbering about two thousand, rushed down the steep bank into the sea, and were drowned in the sea.*

(14) *The swineherds ran off and told it in the city and in*

*the country. Then people came to see what it was that had
happened.* (15) *They came to Jesus and saw the demoniac sitting
there, clothed and in his right mind, the very man who had
had the legion; and they were afraid.* (16) *Those who had seen
what had happened to the demoniac and to the swine reported
it.* (17) *Then they began to beg Jesus to leave their neighborhood.*
(18) *As he was getting into the boat, the man who had been
possessed by demons begged him that he might be with him.*
(19) *But Jesus refused, and said to him, "Go home to your friends,
and tell them how much the Lord has done for you, and what
mercy he has shown you."* (20) *And he went away and began to
proclaim in the Decapolis how much Jesus had done for him;
and everyone was amazed.*

A man possessed by the devil? A demoniac? Here is a story some
people will be very tempted to dismiss, especially those who think
that talk of demonic possession or devils has nothing to teach us, that
demons and devils belong to another time and place. Surely (they
claim all too rationally and reasonably) this is a tale of primitive
superstition, or at least prescientific and precritical thinking. But when
we approach the Scriptures, such condescension is out of place.
Moreover, it would be singularly unfortunate if we overlooked the
lessons this powerful story may provide for all of us.

Mark, the storyteller, places this account immediately after the
incident of the stilling of a storm.[6] That story ended with the words,
"They were filled with great awe and said to one another, 'Who then
is this?'" (Mk 4:41). Mark is, evidently, developing a theme, for the
end of the story we are about to examine concludes in a very similar
way: "Everyone was amazed" (Mk 5:20). Clearly, Jesus is opening many
people's eyes. Will he open ours? People are slowly beginning to understand, to finally "get it." Will we?

Before that storm, Jesus had planned to cross to the other side of
the lake (Mk 4:35). Now, with Peter and the disciples still far from
understanding Jesus' identity, they sail (or row) to the other side, to
the country of the Gerasenes. Once again Jesus is crossing bound-

aries, as he so often does. That is an intrinsic part of his ministry of outreach and encounter. In this particular case, he is reaching out, not to the Chosen People, and not even to the "lost sheep of the House of Israel" (Mt 15:24), but to a pagan people. His ministry of compassion and healing is truly without boundaries.

Jesus is probably very tired at this point, but he will find no respite as long as there are troubled souls and the possibility of encounters that might lead to faith. Suddenly, seemingly out of nowhere, a deranged man appears. He is a "dead man walking," "socially dead,"[7] not living in society, but, precisely, living in the graveyard, where only the dead are to be found. He has no real life at all and is left to his own devices, beyond help and beyond hope. He is virtually dead, he might as well be dead, and he is slowly beating himself to death. What is going on here?

We learn that the people of his village had unsuccessfully tried to bind him, both with chains and fetters or shackles (ankle and foot restraints). The story tells us, rather enigmatically, that "no one could restrain him any more" (v. 4), which is not mentioned in Matthew's or Luke's version. The Jerusalem Bible tells us, "no one had the strength to subdue him." It will become clear in due course that it is probably not brute strength that is the issue here, but *strength of purpose*. Perhaps the people could have contained or confined this man if they had really tried or really put their minds to it, but they did not have the incentive to do so. For whatever reason, they had established a symbiosis, what René Girard[8] called their "cyclic pathology"—a state of mutual, debilitating dependency. As for the demented man, he lived among the tombs and in the mountains—clearly out of the ambit of normal social life—and showed himself to be of two minds (schizophrenic) about his very existence. Yet even though he lived in the graveyard, he would not have been entirely hidden: occasionally, he would have been seen by mourners and burial parties. So, on the one hand, he is living, surviving, and clinging to life; but on the other, he is gradually and with great difficulty killing himself, by autolapidation: stoning himself to death. His behavior is compulsive, addictive, and destructive. It is a grotesque picture and a human tragedy. No wonder he is described as having an unclean spirit, for no one in their right mind would behave in this way. No wonder his erstwhile community appears to be of two minds about him as well.

"When he saw Jesus from afar, he ran and bowed down before him" ("worshipped him," says the Revised Standard Version translation of the Bible) (v. 6). This is quite extraordinary: the man sees Jesus *from afar*, yet clearly he is able to identify him, because he deliberately runs to him and *worships*. A remarkable characteristic of very troubled and suffering people is their capacity to see things other people miss, perceive what is not superficially apparent, and provide deep insight.[9] For this particular man, believed to be possessed by an unclean spirit or demon, the capacity not only to recognize Jesus, but to approach him in an attitude of worship, speaks volumes about his fundamental disposition. On the other hand, we should not overlook Jesus' own magnetism: this man is *drawn* to Jesus.

So when we hear what the man has to say next, we should remember that he is already worshiping Jesus (Luke actually states that he fell down before Jesus). In a loud voice he cries out, from the very depth of his agony, "What have you to do with me, Jesus, Son of the Most High God? I adjure you by God, do not torment me" (v. 7).

Why does he say, "What have you to do with me?" when it is precisely the other way round? It was the deranged man who intentionally came to Jesus, and from quite a distance, too. Jesus may not have had *anything* to do with him had it not been for the man's own dramatic initiative. And to identify Jesus in such a theologically complete and explicit way is quite amazing. Jesus' own disciples are still a long way from this insight. To say "Jesus, Son of the Most High God" shows not only that this man presumes to address Jesus by his first name (which is either a sign of intimacy and perhaps even an indication of an earlier encounter or quite rude and inappropriate), but also that he knows a good deal more than Jesus' name. To address him, unaided, as "Son of the Most High God" is astonishing: it is nothing less than an act, a declaration, of faith.

The troubled man implores Jesus not to torment him. Why? Some commentators have said that he is now speaking with his *other* voice.

Mark has told us that this nameless one has an unclean spirit: that he is not himself. Now, having heard his *authentic* self declare faith in Jesus, we hear his *inauthentic* (out-of-mind, demented, possessed) self speaking out. This is the putative unclean spirit, who simply cannot abide being in the presence of Jesus, and would not be there at all except that his better half had already come to Jesus. This is the most likely explanation, since Jesus immediately responds by directly addressing the unclean spirit: "Come out of the man, you unclean spirit!" (v. 8). Typically, Jesus does not embrace or even touch a person who is distressed and possessed by a spirit: his *healing word* is sufficiently powerful. "Come out" is an order, an imperative. Technically, it is a performative utterance: the command itself has the power to bring about what its words demand. Jesus *is* the Word of life, the Word of God, the Word that changes the world.

Jesus then interrogates the spirit by asking his name. Again, Mark appears to understand the social function of naming very well: to ask for someone's name is to claim to have authority, to have a right to the name. To give one's name is either a sign of freedom or a sign that one is powerless to withhold it. In this case, it is very clearly the latter. Jesus is looking for some identification, some self-disclosure, as he so often does when he encounters a troubled person. The spirit replies, "My name is Legion; for we are many." This is like saying, "Call me Crowd, or Army." The man has no particular name and because he has no particular identity he is lost, neither accountable nor in control.

Interestingly, "Legion" begs not to be sent out of the country, which is very revealing. In societies characterized by possession and possession cults, the possessed person is usually believed either to be controlled by a host or in need of a host, through which to accomplish otherwise impossible acts. Today, people in many cultures believe that the spirits of people who are witches leave the body at night while they are asleep and roam around through the host-body of a bat, or an owl, or some other night creature. In the present case, the demoniac seems to be pleading not to be separated from his host (his twin, his "familiar"), lest he lose the identity he has assumed, and thereby lose his power. This man, identified as "possessed," was truly unfree, imprisoned, in thrall to an alien spirit (in fact a whole Legion of spirits) which had come to take up residence, to possess and control him just as a puppeteer controls a puppet.

No sooner had the spirit spoken through the medium of his host, begging to be sent into some nearby pigs, than Jesus granted this destructive request. Now, the matter was, for all intents and purposes, resolved. Here is the rationale. Legion needs a host in order to subsist. A herd of pigs is rooting nearby, and Legion foolishly asks to have them as hosts: it seems to be the only available choice other than risking destruction by Jesus. But pigs were understood to be unclean or ungodly (and this encounter took place, after all, beyond the land of Israel). Now, Legion's whole existence depends upon disturbing the godly. But swine are already *ungodly*, unclean. So Legion, having entered the pigs, is in an unsustainable environment. He has nothing left to live for, no creatively ungodly work to do and, therefore, no way to continue living. Legion simply cannot survive under these conditions. When there is nothing left to live for, suicide or self-destruction becomes the only way to end the unbearable pain. So the legion of unclean spirits that now has the legion of piggy-hosts—some two thousand, says Mark—promptly rushes to self-destruction through drowning (another typical cultural detail: many spirits appear vulnerable to water).

The demented man, now suddenly transformed because he was made free, clothed (Luke had commented on his nakedness) and in his right mind (and thus "single-minded") is to be found sitting with Jesus in a posture of discipleship. Order has been restored.

The herdsmen had broadcast the news across the city and country, and curious people ("gapers") came to find what excitement they could. But when they saw what had transpired, both the townsfolk and the countryfolk "were afraid" (v. 15). Of course they were! The young man was restored to health and freed of his demons. He was addicted no more. However, his neighbors proved themselves to be anything but free. They were very clearly addicted, both to their ambivalence and lack of commitment to their neighbor, and to their own fears and inaction. They must have sensed that Jesus was very likely to offer to set them free, too. And they could not abide that: better the "unfreedom" you already know than the freedom you don't know. So they actually begged Jesus to leave. They could not live with him, nor with his freedom, nor with his challenge that they find something for which to live. They are accustomed to living in the twilight of life, dependent upon the demented man who has become their scapegoat, claiming that they had done everything within their power to subdue him. In fact, they really have done nothing creative. They may have done everything they could to maintain the status quo, and certainly showed no determination to be rid of their codependency on the poor demented man in their midst.

Jesus is readying himself to leave and, at the last minute, the young man, who has already *come* to Jesus, asks to be allowed to *stay* with Jesus. But the one who has *come* will now be bidden to *go*: the divine imperative becomes the young man's commissioning. He is *sent* home, *sent* to his friends, *sent* to tell the Good News that he had experienced so palpably in his very being. Jesus will leave that place, but not without a witness, not without a healed healer, a rehabilitated addict, a healthy disciple. And the young man, overjoyed at his elevation in status, does Jesus' bidding and begins to proclaim the wonderful works of God to his friends.

But who were his friends, after all this? The text says that he went far beyond his hometown and into the ten cities (the Decapolis). And such is the power of his witness that "everyone was amazed": they finally "got it," they finally understood. The question we are left with is: Do we get it? Do we understand? And there is another question to ponder: Just how many of that man's own community were included in that "everyone," and how many remained locked in their own little world?

Endnotes

6. The more elaborated story of the walking on the water comes after the story of the possessed man. It can be found in Mark

6:45–54. However, we will follow Matthew's more complete account (Mt 14:22–33).

7. We will see social death in more detail in later encounters: the woman with a hemorrhage (Mk 5:25), the bent-over woman (Lk 13:10–17), and elsewhere.

8. René Girard, "The Demons of Gerasa." In *The Scapegoat*. John Hopkins University Press, 1986: 165–184.

9. This is commonplace, understood by anyone who works with mentally ill patients, and should not be dismissed as a popular belief or superstition.

CHAPTER THREE

"Lord, I Am Not Worthy"

(Lk 7:1-10)

(1) *After Jesus had finished all his sayings in the hearing of the people, he entered Capernaum.* (2) *A centurion there had a slave whom he valued highly, and who was ill and close to death.* (3) *When he heard about Jesus he sent some Jewish elders to him, asking him to come and heal his slave.* (4) *When they came to Jesus they appealed to him earnestly, saying, "He is worthy of having you do this for him,* (5) *for he loves our people, and it is he who built our synagogue for us."* (6) *And Jesus went with them, but when he was not far from the house, the centurion sent friends to say to him, "Lord, do not trouble yourself, for I am not worthy to have you come under my roof;* (7) *therefore I did not presume to come to you. But only speak the word, and let my servant be healed.* (8) *For I also am a man set under authority, with soldiers under me; and I say to one, 'Go,' and he goes, and to another, 'Come,' and he comes, and to my slave, 'Do this,' and the slave does it."* (9) *When Jesus heard this he was amazed at him, and turning to the crowd that followed him, he said, "I tell you, not even in Israel have I found such faith."* (10) *When those who had been sent returned to the house, they found the slave in good health.*

S ome phrases are such a part of the English language that we rarely
stop to think about them until, perhaps, we discover that they are
the words of Shakespeare, or Homer, or even the Bible. They are such
a part of our lives, we may simply not have consciously thought about
either their origins or their original context. The story about the
centurion, told to us by Luke, has in it such phrases which have become
part of our religious culture: phrases like, "Lord, I am not worthy,"
and "but only speak the word." We may be surprised when we learn
more about their origin, and even learn more about an encounter
that never actually happened.

We have already seen in Chapter One, a meeting that took place
at Capernaum concerning the healing of the paralytic (Mk 2:1–12).
Jesus was an itinerant preacher, which meant that he was constantly
on the move. Because of this characteristic, it is permissible to take
the literary liberty of switching to the story about the Gerasene country and the man who lived there (Mk 5:1–20), without evident dis-
continuity in the present book. Now we return to Capernaum, for yet
another story about that town. But this is from a different storyteller:
we are in the Gospel of Luke, who has a soft spot for outsiders and a
passion for outreach, inclusion, and mission.

Up to this point in Luke's narrative, Jesus has moved from Nazareth to Capernaum. In Nazareth, he had opened the scroll and read
his own "job description" from the prophet Isaiah. Then, having met
with immediate approval, he saw this approval turn to hostility and
outrage as his own people turned against him (Lk 4:16–30). Now in
Capernaum, he has been healing people, including Peter's mother-
in-law and the paralyzed man whose friends brought him to Jesus.
He has also called the first of his apostles and begun discussing theological questions with anyone who appears interested (Lk 4:31—6:16).
He has spoken to a great crowd, using the phrases we now call the "Be-
atitudes," telling people they were "happy," even though many were by
no means convinced of that fact. He warned them about hypocrisy and
judging others (Lk 6:17–45), and urged them to follow his teachings
and not to just follow the crowd which was growing around him.

The story about the centurion begins when Jesus returns to

Capernaum after all this teaching (Lk 7:1). No sooner has his party arrived than a delegation of Jewish elders approaches Jesus. They were sent by a Roman centurion who does not himself appear. The centurion is clearly an outsider, a servant of Rome, a military man, charged with keeping the peace and watching out for sedition. In order to have this position, we assume he must have been a capable man, someone of authority. Many such people were also authoritarian and brutal. But this unnamed person is different.

It is always interesting to speculate about the identity of certain people. In the case of these stories from Scripture, we come to wonder why some people are named and others are not. We will see several instances of unnamed people of some consequence, and others of named people who seem to be of little consequence (even including some of the Twelve, the closest companions of Jesus). This particular man's identity is suggested to us by his occupation and status: he is a centurion, a man with a hundred soldiers under his command, an individual with a significant household depending upon him. He also has friends among the Jewish elders, and it is these persons who act as corporate go-betweens on his behalf.

The very fact that this centurion has Jewish friends speaks highly of his openness and tolerance, and also of his commitment not simply to remain an alien outsider and a representative of a foreign power, but to become a participating outsider, someone who is genuinely involved in the social life of the local people. These selected friends are not just hangers-on; they offer sincere testimonies on behalf of the centurion: he is "worthy," "he loves the people," and he actually built their synagogue (vv. 4–5). It is interesting to note here that Luke has just explained that Jesus made a point of calling people to positive action and not simply to uttering pious platitudes (Lk 6:46–49). Obviously, the centurion is an exemplary person in this respect.

He is also a compassionate and worried man. One of his slaves is dying. Instead of just replacing the ill slave, which he could so easily have done, he frets and worries, taking action to get him help. The centurion must already have done what he could for this highly valued slave (v. 2), but to no avail. Now he has heard that Jesus has returned to

Capernaum, the centurion seems to have no hesitation at all. He sends his friends on a mission of mercy to Jesus.

The scene is set and, although the centurion is physically absent from the picture, evidently Jesus is persuaded to help because of the man's reputation, both for good deeds and compassion. The narrative says simply, "and Jesus went with them" (v. 6). This will not be the last time that Jesus will adopt the position of the follower, allowing others to lead. He is the Teacher who not only proclaims that the first shall be last and that the master shall be the servant: he exemplifies it. Does Jesus go with them because he is persuaded by the centurion's good deeds? He has, after all, built a synagogue and won the respect of a Jewish community. Or does Jesus follow just because someone is in need and because Jesus is no respecter of persons? The person in need, of course, is not the centurion himself, but a lowly servant, a virtual nonentity. But it is for such as these that Jesus came: as John Dominic Crossan explicitly states, Jesus came for the "nobodies" of society.

But Jesus never actually encountered the slave. Before he even reached the centurion's house, another group of friends came to inform Jesus that the centurion had not actually expected Jesus to go all the way to his house, but only to speak a healing word.

For several reasons, this is extraordinary behavior. In the first place, the centurion seems to have an unlimited number of friends who can be sent to do his bidding at any time. Moreover, these friends even seem to be quite happy to do so. This man must really have made some very good friends. Second, it now becomes clear that not only is Jesus unlikely to meet the sick slave, he is just as unlikely to meet the centurion himself. But the latter's behavior is not rude, even if it appears to be so; he is simply modest and humble of heart. It is certainly not his intention to appear rude, as his spokespersons make clear. Quite simply, he feels unworthy to have Jesus come into his house. His reason for sending others to do his bidding had nothing to do with his own high estate, and everything to do with his own honest self-understanding: compared to Jesus, he too was a nobody.

Here we have a richly significant scenario: Jesus looking for an encounter with two self-conscious nobodies, yet unable to make contact with either of them because of the protocol that has spontaneously sprouted up around the developing situation.

There is surely no Christian who is not familiar with the words, "Lord, I am not worthy to have you come under my roof" (v. 6), because we have all made them become our own in the intimate moment of our reception of Holy Communion. Nor are we unaware that these are the words of a centurion who wanted to have his slave healed, but did not want to trouble Jesus unduly. Few of us may realize, though, that these words do not come to us directly from the lips of the centurion himself, and Jesus and the centurion never actually meet.

It was the centurion's friends who carried his message. These friends were the ones who uttered the words "Lord, I am not worthy" on behalf of the centurion. The master himself remains at home. The remainder of his statement, as well, was relayed only through indirect or reported speech, not as words placed on the centurion's own lips. The friends tell us what he said, "...I did not presume to come to you. But only speak the word, and let my servant be healed" (v. 7).

He did not presume to come, because he identified Jesus, not only as "Lord," but as much more than that: as someone who could snatch his slave from death. Not only did he not presume to come to Jesus, he simply did not imagine that Jesus needed to come to him either. The phrase, "But only speak the word, and let my servant be healed" (v. 7) was what he told his spokesmen to say. (Or in cadences that may be more familiar to us, "Say but the word and my servant will be healed.") This man understood that Jesus had the power of the spoken word, that he spoke a word that could actually change things, that his word was truly a *performative* word. The centurion was expressing his faith in the person of Jesus and, at the same time, in the very word of Jesus. It may be an inchoate theology, but it is truly amazing nevertheless. Later believers would see Jesus as the *logos*, the Eternal Divine Word-made-flesh, living among us: God's creative uttering forth. But this centurion has beaten everyone to the finish line: he has actually put this mystery into his own words, and they still echo today, after two thousand years. They are formidable, faith-filled, and unforgettable. And yet we only have them secondhand, reported by the centurion's friends.

The centurion's message continues, all the time in reported speech. He says, "For I also am a man set under authority, with soldiers under me; and I say to one, 'Go,' and he goes, and to another, 'Come,' and he comes, and to my slave, 'Do this,' and the slave does it" (v. 8). He concludes that what applies to his own life, the issuing of commands in the certain knowledge that they will be carried out, applies, *a fortiori*, to this Jesus whose activities have come to his notice. The centurion does not simply believe what has been said about Jesus, he believes in Jesus himself. In other words, he has faith. He is inspired to put his belief, his trust, even his reputation, on the line for Jesus. He is utterly confident that as he can bring about change by the imperial authority of his centurion's word, so Jesus can change the world by the other-worldly authority of his own word.

This exhibition is quite amazing, and we are given absolutely no indication of how the centurion came to this depth of faith. Certainly he is unusual in that he passes through no discernible stages of faith: from the moment we encounter him, he seems utterly convinced. But it is instructive also to notice Jesus' reaction. He is just as surprised as we are. He too is "amazed," so much so that he turns to the crowd and spontaneously shares his amazement with them: "…not even in Israel have I found such faith" (v. 9). This would not be the last time we hear that phrase from him, for his boundary-crossing journeys will not only lead him to encounters with people looking for faith and growing in faith, but they will lead him to further amazement at the full-blown faith he encounters where he least expects it.

The final, remarkable fact in this story is that this powerful encounter between Jesus and the centurion, an encounter that is among the most familiar as well as the most memorable of all the encounters in the New Testament, was not a physical encounter at all; the centurion was at home the entire time. But, in spite of that, it was, nonetheless, a true encounter; it was an encounter in faith. "Blessed are those who have not seen and yet have come to believe," said Jesus to Thomas much later (Jn 20:29). This centurion would not have needed to be reminded; he already knew, from experience, the truth of what Jesus told Thomas and the rest of us as well.

CHAPTER FOUR

A Man's Request, A Woman's Resolve

(Mk 5:21–43)[10]

(21) *When Jesus had crossed again in the boat to the other side, a great crowd gathered around him; and he was by the sea.* (22) *Then one of the leaders of the synagogue named Jairus came and, when he saw him, fell at his feet* (23) *and begged him repeatedly, "My little daughter is at the point of death. Come and lay your hands on her, so that she may be made well, and live."* (24) *So he went with him.*

And a large crowd followed him and pressed in on him. (25) *Now there was a woman who had been suffering from hemorrhages for twelve years.* (26) *She had endured much under many physicians, and had spent all that she had; and she was no better, but rather grew worse.* (27) *She had heard about Jesus, and came up behind him in the crowd and touched his cloak,* (28) *for she said, "If I but touch his clothes, I will be made well."* (29) *Immediately her hemorrhage stopped; and she felt in her body that she was healed of her disease.* (30) *Immediately aware that power had gone forth from him, Jesus turned about in the crowd and said, "Who touched my clothes?"* (31) *And his disciples said to him, "You see the crowd pressing in on you; how can you say, 'Who touched me?'"* (32) *He looked all around to see who had done it.* (33) *But the woman, knowing what had happened to her, came in fear and trembling, fell down before him, and told him the whole truth.* (34) *He said to her, "Daughter, your faith has made you well; go in peace, and be healed of your disease."*

(35) *While he was still speaking, some people came from the leader's house to say, "Your daughter is dead. Why trouble the teacher any further?"* (36) *But overhearing what they said, Jesus said to the leader of the synagogue, "Do not fear, only believe."* (37) *He allowed no one to follow him except Peter, James, and John, the brother of James.* (38) *When they came to the house of the leader of the synagogue, he saw a commotion, people weeping and wailing loudly.* (39) *When he had entered, he said to them, "Why do you make a commotion and weep?" The child is not dead but sleeping."* (40) *And they laughed at him. Then he put them all outside, and took the child's father and mother and those who were with him, and went in where the child was.* (41) *He took her by the hand and said to her, "Talitha cum," which means, "Little girl, get up!"* (42) *And immediately the girl got up and began to walk about (she was twelve years of age). At this they were overcome with amazement.* (43) *He strictly ordered them that no one should know this, and told them to give her something to eat.*

Matthew, Mark, and Luke all tell this story-within-a-story (a "sandwich," or an *intercalation*), so its construction and presentation should tell us something significant. First, there is an encounter between Jesus and a man named Jairus. But before that story concludes, another encounter takes place. The second encounter between Jesus and a nameless woman runs its course. Then finally we return for the conclusion of the story of Jairus.

Immediately after liberating the man living in the graveyard, and perhaps some of his community as well, Jesus was coming away from Gerasene country. But despite his works of power not everyone was drawn to him. Indeed, the local people had actually begged Jesus to leave them. Perversely, some people seem more comfortable living with their demons: it gives them something to complain about and allows them to avoid their own responsibilities. As a result, Jesus is again on the move and becoming something of a celebrity, for "a great crowd gathered round him" (v. 21). But he is now on his own side of the lake, back in Jewish territory. Perhaps he will find the faith he is seeking.

Jesus does not appear to have a plan but is simply and clearly available to the people. Our story begins as a synagogue official bursts through the crowd and throws himself at Jesus' feet. It may be reminiscent of another, later story: of the rich young man who stopped Jesus by a similar tactic. This older man "fell at his feet," or "fell prostrate," (Mk 5:22); the young man "knelt before him" (in other translations, "fell on his knees" [10:17]); and we have just heard about the mentally ill man from Gerasa who "ran and bowed down before him" (or "worshipped him," RSV) (Mk 5:6).

Jairus neither worships, nor comes to dispute or argue theology, though he does fall at the feet of Jesus in a very respectful gesture. His agenda is simple and very urgent: his little daughter seems to be at the point of death and he feels utterly powerless. Jairus has nothing to lose, yet his request is by no means hopeless or despairing, and this fact will prove critical. "Come and lay your hands on her, so that she may be made well, and live" (v. 23), he begs. He seems to know that *if* Jesus lays his hands on the girl, *then* she will live. Here is a man of faith; and faith, as we discover from these stories, makes miracles.

The text says, "So Jesus went with him" ("followed him" [in the Jerusalem Bible] (v. 24). We may notice that Jesus has not only responded *immediately* but has adopted the role of *follower*. In another interesting reversal of roles, Jairus leads, Jesus follows, and they hurry to his home. Here Jesus is exemplifying what he talks about so often: the leader must become the follower, just as the first must become the last, the master must become the servant, and the teacher must become the learner. At the core of the Gospel is a series of reversals, and Jesus exemplifies them all. There must be no clinging to status nor lording it over others. So Jesus follows Jairus. But just when we are being drawn deeply into this story, and perhaps pondering this curious fact, there is a sudden interruption.

"There was a woman" (v. 25). She did not interrupt in the same way Jairus did, but she was *there*. Later, we will see another case of a woman who was *there* when Jesus was teaching.[11] There is something compelling about them: they are women, and therefore socially insignificant; but *they are there*, and therefore physically unavoidable. This woman has a similar strategy to Jairus. He had indicated that if Jesus were to come, his daughter would live; the woman believed that if she only touched his clothes, then she would be well. This if/then logic is enough to drive the woman into action.

This woman's story is both interesting and pathetic. She had suffered under the care of many physicians, spent all her money, and yet was worse off than when she started. It appears that she is a socially isolated and, perhaps, even an abandoned woman. Maybe her husband and family could not cope with her or her chronic illness. Maybe the fact that she consulted doctors was itself offensive to some people: the Scriptures did warn people not to consort with doctors, but to put their faith in God.[12] So maybe she was living under a dark cloud. She was also impoverished by her pursuit of professional assistance, which may have been enough to convince some people that indeed she had no faith in God. More than that: her condition had actually worsened. Some medical conditions (called *iatrogenic* diseases) are actually caused by the circumstances in which people seek a cure: caused by hospitals or doctors, or by the prescribed treatment itself. This woman had nowhere else to go: neither to husband, nor to savings, nor to medicine.

But she had *heard* about Jesus, and she was *there*. She was faithful. Having heard, she had listened and understood. Jesus often spoke about those who had ears but did not hear, and appealed to the people to listen to what he said.

For the people of that time, any definition of the word "human" would have included two essential features: ears to comprehend and being capable of walking upright on two feet. Both of these characteristics are featured in this story as Jesus subtly teaches his lesson. Human beings have a unique capacity to internalize, to hear, to listen, and to act upon another person's speech. This woman is portrayed as truly human, despite her obvious physical limitations. And those who are not only *there* but who also *hear* are among the closest disciples of Jesus. By contrast, some people are not fully present, and not fully attentive. Jesus is often critical of those who have ears but do not listen and fail to hear: they are not behaving in a fully human way.

This woman has no name, but more important she has no life. Being ritually unclean (hemorrhaging) for twelve years has separated her from people. She is socially dead if not physically dead. To be avoided by everyone is to be rendered utterly isolated. Social death—effective ostracism such as that experienced by the Gerasene demoniac in chapter 5 of the Gospel of Mark—can be almost as real as physical death. Whoever is socially dead might almost, as well, be physically dead, because life can be unbearable in social isolation.

This "dead" woman's faith will restore her to life. But first she will be exposed to the public gaze, will publicly give witness to her faith, and will be publicly commended by Jesus. Her faith was strong enough to help her overcome the perception that she was as good as dead, yet she was afraid because her religion declared her ritually contaminated. She may have been in the same position as certain people we know: officially excluded from participation in religion (the sacraments) because of some legal irregularity, but determined to have access at least to the Eucharist, the food of life. She may have been excluded from the synagogue but determined to encounter Jesus, as a way to short-circuit religious regulations. She was playing a dangerous game but she was willing to take the risk. She believed that all she had to do was to touch Jesus, unobserved.

The very moment she touched him, two things happened. *Immediately* she felt herself healed; and, at the same moment, Jesus felt depleted. Her gain was, in some sense, his loss. Before she could move, much less melt into the crowd, Jesus called out "who touched my clothes?" (v. 30). She must have been dumbfounded as her plan began to unravel. The disciples distracted Jesus for an instant, yet even before he made eye contact with her, she came forward. Despite her fear and shaking, this was a woman of integrity. No prevarication for her. No attempt to lie or justify herself. No sooner had she been discovered than she "told him the whole truth" (v. 33).

Such strength of character is astounding. Nothing would stop her from reaching Jesus, and nothing could persuade her to lie. In an instant she becomes a public witness to her faith: the word *martyr* describes precisely who she is and what she does. Her courage is acknowledged and rewarded by Jesus, who calls her "my daughter,"[13] tells her that indeed her faith has made a miracle, and sends her off in peace: no more fear or trembling, no more worry about being among the living dead, no more guilt about trying to find a way through the religious rules that held her bound tightly. She was free: finally, totally free.

Jesus has taught a profound lesson. Not only has he healed a woman of faith, he has given the lie to bad theology. God does *not* want death, but life. Jesus would demonstrate that to be touched by a ritually defiled person was *not* to transfer contamination. Perhaps, more forcibly put, to be touched by a holy person was indeed to transfer holiness or healing to the defiled one: this is "reverse contamination." Jesus was committed to doing holy things, to making things and people holy—even, we might say, to "contaminating" people with his own holy goodness. The depletion he felt was his own sensitivity to the outflowing of godly power. We know how his labors tired him, and how he needed to be alone in prayer in order to be filled and replenished. This is a lesson for us to learn, and a reminder not to imagine that we help or heal by our own power. The union between a person and God is a measure of that person's godliness.

Hardly has the woman been sent on her way than the first, unfinished story picks up again and moves toward its climax. Jairus is suddenly confronted by a delegation of people from his home, reporting that his daughter has died. Curiously, however, Jesus rather pointedly ignores the remark and offers words of encouragement: "Do not fear, only believe" (v. 36). Jairus has just seen belief-in-action, and its power to overcome fear, as he witnessed the encounter between the woman and Jesus. Therefore, he should not find Jesus' instructions beyond his understanding. But the text says nothing about his reaction; all we know is that along with Jesus and his three closest disciples Jairus hurries back home. But this time the roles are reversed: Jesus leads and Jairus follows.

By the time they arrived, the conventional weeping and wailing had already begun. This culturally institutionalized behavior is sometimes rather exaggerated and almost impossible to stop. The wailing tends to become almost infectious and very, very loud. So Jesus had to raise his voice as he entered the house and declared that the girl was simply sleeping. They were right to laugh: no one would have been able to sleep through that noisy keening and ululating.

Going directly to the girl, but accompanied now by her mother as well as her father and the three disciples, Jesus immediately made physical contact: taking her by the hand, he spoke to her. These are not words of command or authority, but lilting words of gentle encouragement in babylike language, supported by physical affection and encouragement. Jesus used the local dialect, an intimate form of speech, and barely even grammatical in form: exactly the language a gentle, loving parent would use to awaken a child from a deep sleep.[14]

Immediately the little girl got up. This is the third time the word *immediately* is used, and it will occur once more: "Immediately they were overcome with amazement" (v. 42). In each case, we are struck by the speed with which things happen, and with the responsiveness of Jesus. Mark the storyteller loves to use this word as an indication of just how responsive Jesus could be, and just how effective his response was. The little girl got up in an instant and walked. Walking is that other particularly human attribute: this was no apparition, but a flesh-and-blood human being who was doing the walking. The story adds that she was twelve years old, neatly linking her with the story of the sick woman. That woman had been afflicted for twelve years and was socially dead; on this very day her life began. By contrast, the girl had only lived for twelve short years and then died; on this very day her life ended. She had not even begun to live as an adult woman: now, thanks to Jesus, she was given the fullness of adult life. The older woman had also been brought back to life in a profoundly significant way: not only was she restored to physical health but her social identity as an adult woman had been restored.

The story ends with two deeply significant statements. Jesus warned the people not to broadcast this event (people attracted by the miraculous do not necessarily have the faith that Jesus is seeking). He told the family to give the girl something to eat (emphasizing that she is a real, physical person, not a ghost; and also involving the family and the community in her rehabilitation).

This last point is critically important. We need to understand that Jesus has come to involve everyone in the work of the Kingdom, or the Realm of God. The very next chapter of Mark's Gospel tells the story of the feeding of the five thousand. The disciples cannot cope with the crowd, and their immediate reaction is to ask Jesus to send the people away to fend for themselves. But Jesus says: "You give them something to eat" (Mk 6:37). Here, in this story, after raising the little girl, Jesus says the very same thing. This suggests two things to us: first, Jesus acknowledges that the girl's family, the disciples (we ourselves) have the capacity to make a difference in particular situations of need; and, second, we also are not without some resources of our own, some nourishment, if only we dig deep and share. Whether we are facing situations of physical hunger, or even the eucharistic famine that affects so many Christian communities today, we must not simply pray for miracles, but remember that, in the face of the great need of our sisters and brothers, we can and we must "give them something to eat [our]selves."

Endnotes

10. See also Matthew 9:18–26 and Luke 8:40–56.
11. See the story of the bent-over woman in Luke 13:10–17.
12. See 2 Chronicles 6:12. The illustration is perhaps a warning against idolatry as much as against medicine. Nevertheless, Israel, when compared with its neighbors (notably Egypt), had a very rudimentary understanding of health and disease.
13. If Jesus calls her "my daughter," and if he is a "Son of Abraham," then she is a daughter of Abraham. This is an enormously important identity marker. Jesus bestows the title explicitly upon Zacchaeus, and also explicitly calls the bent-over woman a daughter of Abraham (Lk 13:16).
14. Even today, in Malta, the people use virtually this same expression. The Maltese language is a cognate of Aramaic.

CHAPTER FIVE

"Lord, Save Me!"

(Mt 14:22–33)[15]

(22) *Immediately he [Jesus] made the disciples get into the boat and go on ahead to the other side, while he dismissed the crowds. (23) And after he had dismissed the crowds, he went up the mountain by himself to pray. When evening came, he was there alone, (24) but by this time the boat, battered by the waves, was far from the land, for the wind was against them. (25) And early in the morning he came walking toward them on the sea. (26) But when the disciples saw him walking on the sea, they were terrified, saying, "It is a ghost!" And they cried out in fear. (27) But immediately Jesus spoke to them and said, "Take heart, it is I; do not be afraid."*

(28) Peter answered him, "Lord, if it is you, command me to come to you on the water." (29) He said, "Come." So Peter got out of the boat, started walking on the water, and came toward Jesus. (30) But when he noticed the strong wind, he became frightened, and beginning to sink, he cried out, "Lord, save me!" (31) Jesus immediately reached out his hand and caught him, saying to him, "You of little faith, why did you doubt?" (32) When they got into the boat, the wind ceased. (33) And those in the boat worshiped him, saying, "Truly you are the Son of God."

By all accounts, Peter was a larger-than-life figure: exuberant to the point of impetuosity, bold to the point of recklessness, moody to the point of depression, confident to the point of arrogance, and contrite to the point of wretchedness. These characteristics are only a few indications of his range and complexity. Above all perhaps, he lives in the memory not simply as the leader of the apostles but as the one who best epitomizes *Everyman.* He may even appeal to women because of some of the *anima* qualities he displays: faithfulness, persistence, and willingness to try again.

Matthew's Gospel tells the story of Peter's dramatic near-death experience in a way that does not spare Peter's blushes. Mark's story is more diplomatic, omitting Peter's escapade and Jesus' gentle remonstration. In Matthew's hands, the story contains some important details that help us understand and sympathize with Peter: perhaps Peter is not all that different from us, not an impossible role model.

On this occasion, Peter, representative of the Twelve, comes to faith in Jesus in three steps.[16] The first, or the starting point, is the way Jesus is perceived: he is identified as "a ghost" (by everyone in the boat). In a second movement, Peter himself identifies Jesus as "Lord" (twice). The third step takes place when Peter (with the group speaking in unison) makes an act of faith in Jesus as "Son of God," which anticipates Thomas's even more explicit act of faith after the Resurrection: "My Lord and my God!" (Jn 20:28). But, first, let us look at the story and the encounter.

The immediate aftermath of the feeding of the five thousand is the context for this encounter. On that occasion, Jesus had thrown down a very significant challenge. In response to the disciples' rather peevish request to send the hungry people away, he had told them to "give them something to eat yourselves" in the words of the Jerusalem Bible) (14:16). The disciples were becoming lazy and selfish, and Jesus wanted to call upon them to make some personal and collective effort. They hardly rose to that particular occasion, though: Jesus accepted the loaves and fish they had and simply took over.

In both Matthew's and Mark's accounts, it was immediately after the miracle of the loaves that Jesus "made the disciples get into the boat and go on ahead to the other side" (Mt 14:22). Perhaps he was testing them, giving them some time on their own, to see if they could look after themselves and complete a simple sailing trip. After all, they were fishermen, and it was a straightforward enough assignment. Perhaps, he wanted them to have the opportunity to ponder and discuss the events that had just transpired.

Neither Matthew's nor Mark's account gives any indication of the disciples' disposition or conversation. Instead, both accounts turn to Jesus, who "went up the mountain by himself to pray" (v. 23). Evidently he needed this respite and some time for restoration, after his depleting deed of power. In any event, the narrative has established the physical distance between Jesus and the disciples, and the indications are that he wanted it that way. So he was not simply "setting up" the disciples for conversion and a dramatic rescue at sea. Meanwhile, the boat was being "battered by the waves" (v. 24), and "they were straining against the oars against an adverse wind" ("worn out with rowing" in the Jerusalem Bible) (Mk 6:48). The cause of the turbulent waves and the tiredness of the crew was the wind: "The wind was against them" (v. 24).

On three occasions in this story, we will notice the power of the wind and its relationship to the sailors. But if we recall the wind or *ru'ach* that blew over the void in the Creation story (Gen 1:2), we may consider it as a figure of the spirit or, even more explicitly, the Spirit of God. Perhaps, the evangelist is making a subtle point: it was not so much that the wind was against them, *but they were against the wind* (Spirit). By the third intervention of the wind however, we will see that they were no longer struggling, either with the wind or with the Spirit. They were now at peace.

On this first occasion it appears that the disciples and the wind were at odds: they could make no progress and were in serious danger of foundering. Jesus came to them, *from the same direction* as the wind (the wind was blowing at them; Jesus was coming towards them). But if they were distressed by this headwind, they were even more distressed by the appearance of Jesus. Not surprisingly, they failed to recognize him: it was dark, turbulent, and the spray-blown wind lashed at their faces. But, more important, walking on the water was not something even Jesus had done before. Given their cultural context, they thought they were seeing a ghost. Jesus was clearly unrecognizable at first; they were not even sure the figure had physical substance.

The storyteller identifies their fearful cries and the instantaneous response of Jesus: "*Immediately* Jesus spoke to them and said, 'Take heart, it is I; do not be afraid'" (Mt 14:26). Such a dramatic and heartening response. Jesus does not leave his people in abject terror, but responds immediately and speaks encouraging words in a recognizable voice. "Take heart; it is I; do not be afraid": a triple encouragement. First, he speaks words of affirmation; second, words of self-disclosure; and third, words of encouragement. "Take heart" implies "you can do it"; "It is I" evokes "I Am Who I Am"; "Do not be afraid" promises "I am with you."

This self-disclosure on the part of Jesus—"It is I"—seems to be what enables Peter to recognize the true identity of what he first thinks is a ghost. But Peter does not seem to have recognized the classic formula itself (the "*ego eimi*: it is I") in the words of Jesus, to what seems to have been happening. Perhaps Peter simply *knew* it was Jesus because he recognized Jesus' distinctive voice (that is how Mary Magdalen recognized him after the Resurrection: when he called her by her name [Jn 19:16]). But there is another factor. When someone says "It's me," the implication is that we *already* know the voice in question. Whether Peter *saw* that it was Jesus or not, he *knew* that it was he, because the voice was clearly the voice of Jesus. One of the ways people come to faith is by coming to recognize divinity in its many different forms, even when it has been staring them in the face the whole time.

It has been said that the phrase "Do not be afraid" occurs three hundred sixty-five times in the Bible: one for every day of the year. Perhaps, but there are certainly many occasions when people who love God are afraid, and it is comforting to know about God's abiding encouragement. Perhaps the lesson is that it is all right to be afraid, initially. Fear is a rather normal response. But fear is not supposed to paralyze us. It can and must be overcome. We can break through fear and come to peace. And God is at pains constantly to assure us of this.

Impetuous Peter: one moment he is cowering, the next foolhardy.

"Lord, if it is you, command me come to you on the water," he declares (v. 28). He identifies Jesus as "Lord." Clearly, he has recognized Jesus' voice, but Peter is also now addressing Jesus with great respect. Perhaps that is in his best interest, as he is still in serious need of help. Yet Peter seems emboldened. He asks to be invited out of the boat and on to the water. From where does this sudden courage, or foolishness, come? Is it not from an instinct deep inside Peter, an instinct that does not simply propel him into the waves but makes him ask for a sign, an invitation, a call? Peter senses that if he is called then he will also be enabled. Perhaps it is this same instinct, so sure in Peter, that marks him as the "Rock." And Jesus, with breathtaking simplicity, directness, and a challenge, says, "Come." Now Peter's impetuosity will indeed be tested to the fullest extent.

To his great credit, Peter is as quick to get out of the boat as Jesus was to invite him to do so.[17] Peter's downfall is not only due to his taking his eyes off Jesus. He was actually walking on the water for a moment, but then *he saw the wind*. And here it is again: the wind. Of course Peter did not see the wind, as much as he perceived it, sensed it, felt its power.[18] He felt the wind was against him.

Knowing that he was at odds with the wind, Peter was now afraid, and because of this fear he began to sink (Mt 14:30). This is the second time the wind has been against Peter, or vice versa. It will not be until the third time that we understand the effect of being at cross-purposes with the designs of God. Why did Peter feel the wind's strength in this way? Perhaps because he was almost beginning to enjoy his daredevil escapade, and he forgot his total dependency on God. He soon knew better, because he began to sink. Of course, since "the wind" was against him, and also since he was attempting something that was physically impossible, he was indeed going to sink. In that storm, which was still raging, he would most probably drown.

Peter's instincts are no less sure a second time. He cries out, "Lord, save me!" He knows that his only chance for safety and salvation is through the one he recognizes as Jesus and Lord. And true to form, Jesus "immediately reached out his hand and caught him" (Mt 14:31). It is a powerfully tender moment. Peter is safe in Jesus.

But the moment of rescue is also a moment of gentle remonstration: "You of little faith, why did you doubt?" (v. 31). It is gentle because Jesus addresses Peter in the vocative: "[O] you of little faith."
There is no condemnation here. Yet it remonstrates because Peter needs
to be reminded that faith makes miracles and that lack of faith leads nowhere. But now Peter is with Jesus, safe; and Jesus is with Peter, safety.

Jesus gets into the boat, whereupon "the wind ceased" (v. 32).
There was no need for contrary winds now: Peter was not fighting
against God, God's Spirit, or the *ru'ach*; he was at one with Jesus, with
God, and thus with the waves and the elements.

Matthew says that those in the boat worshiped him [Jesus]. It's a
nice conclusion; but they have a long way yet to go before they are
capable of mature worship. It is a start, though. Their instinct to worship, to fall on their knees and reach out to a higher power, also indicates their keen awareness that walking on the water is impossible.
Nevertheless, disciples will indeed be called to do the impossible. If
they are both courageous and faithful they will succeed. But if they
should take their eyes off Jesus and fight against the wind (the inspi-
ration of God), then they will surely sink.

"Truly you are the Son of God" (v. 33) is a lesson learned on the
lake that day, not only by Peter but by at least some of the disciples. It
is a lesson we all need to remember when the weather worsens, when
the winds whip up, when we seem to sense a ghostly presence that
makes us afraid, and when we cry out from the depths, hoping God
will answer.

Endnotes

15. As told in Mark 6:45–52. I used the Matthew text because it
    contains some significant details that have been omitted from
    the more streamlined Marcan version, specifically with respect
    to the chief protagonist, Peter.

16. The step-by-step movement to faith is explained in the Preface.

17. Mark may have remembered the incident, if he was there
    (references to the presences of the "apostles" and "disciples" are

not entirely consistent). Nevertheless, Mark maintains a discreet silence, perhaps saving Peter's blushes. Matthew is not so circumspect.

18. The verb is *blepein*, which translates as "perceive," as much as "see," in a visual sense.

CHAPTER SIX

Crumbs of Comfort

(Mt 15:21–28)[19]

(21) *Jesus left that place [Gennesaret] and went away to the district of Tyre and Sidon.* (22) *Just then a Canaanite woman from that region came out and started shouting, "Have mercy on me, Lord, Son of David; my daughter is tormented by a demon."* (23) *But he did not answer her at all. And his disciples came and urged him, saying, "Send her away, for she keeps shouting after us."* (24) *He answered, "I was sent only to the lost sheep of the house of Israel."* (25) *But she came and knelt before him, saying, "Lord, help me."* (26) *He answered, "It is not fair to take the children's food and throw it to the dogs."* (27) *She said, "Yes, Lord, yet even the dogs eat the crumbs that fall from their masters' table."* (28) *Then Jesus answered her, "Woman, great is your faith! Let it be done for you as you wish." And her daughter was healed instantly.*

Jesus was often besieged by crowds, sometimes for hours on end and occasionally well into the evening (Mt 14:15). There were certainly times when he was "bone-tired" ("the Son of Man has nowhere to lay his head" [Mt 8:20]) and tired people can sometimes be short-tempered or impatient. Their behavior can then be explained and perhaps even excused by their tiredness. But when we try to apply this to Jesus we immediately encounter problems. Generations of believers who have a keen sense of the divinity of Christ may have a difficult time reconciling divinity with tiredness, or Godhead with

39

impatience. A *high Christology* refers to a perception of Jesus that never loses sight of his divinity. A *low Christology* tries to remember that Jesus was human, that "…being found in human form, he humbled himself…" (Phil 2:7–8). The story of the Canaanite woman in Matthew's Gospel is rather resistant to a high-Christology, but very revealing to those who approach it with a low-Christology.

The setting in Matthew's Gospel is quite interesting. Jesus had recently heard of the execution of John the Baptist, his mentor and friend. He tried to find time to be alone and grieve, but was spied by the crowds who followed him in large numbers. Feeling sorry for them, Jesus changed his plans (not something a high Christology can handle very well). There ensued the feeding of the five thousand (Mt 14:13–21). Immediately afterwards, once again Jesus tried to find time to be alone. He sent the disciples ahead of him by boat while he went off to pray, but a sudden storm blew up. The disciples started to panic, and again Jesus' plans had to be changed in order to save the hapless sailors. There followed the episode of the walking on the water (Mt 14:22–33) that we have just explored in Chapter Five.

No sooner had they come to land at Gennesaret, however, than they are again besieged by throngs of people bringing their sick. So Jesus cures many of their sick and then becomes embroiled in an argument with some Pharisees about purity and pollution (Mt 14:34; 15:20). Finally he is free, but evidently even more tired and depleted than before. He tries to escape by making for the region of Tyre and Sidon—"pagan" territory—where he could hope to be undisturbed. But this was not to be.

A woman suddenly burst on the scene, shouting as she did so, and making something of a public spectacle. She did not appear to be a crazy person and was not shouting abuse. She was however a Canaanite, in other words an unbelieving foreigner. She was also a woman and, therefore, considered to be socially insignificant and probably quite used to being ignored. But on this occasion she was loud, and at least, she clearly had no intention of being ignored.

Three things must have caught Jesus' attention, despite his tiredness. First, without any preamble, she called him "Lord," and "Son of

David." Then she asked him to have pity on her. And, finally, her request was not for herself at all: she was pleading on behalf of another person, her daughter.

To call him "Lord" might simply indicate she knew her place or perhaps that she sought to flatter the teacher ("Sir" is how she addresses him in the Jerusalem Bible). But to call him "Son of David" was a different matter. This was the type of honorific title that she could hardly be expected to know, and certainly not to use. It might have been more appropriate on the lips of Jesus himself.[20] She was acknowledging that he came from a royal line and perhaps even more: the Jews were certainly expecting the future messiah to come from David's line. So, her opening gambit, "Lord, Son of David," was very impressive and quite surprising. But she has only just begun.

In the very same breath, the Canaanite woman implores: "Have mercy on me" (v. 22) ("take pity on me" in the Jerusalem Bible). She is seeking compassion from someone who appears to be a complete stranger. The Greek word for compassion is highly significant, indicating the intestines or internal organs. But in Hebrew the word relates more specifically to physical movement and more explicitly to the womb. In the Hebrew Bible it is used about God, though it is clearly a female attribute.[21] What does this woman know? What does she hope to gain? What does she *believe*? Evidently, she believes, at the very least, that Jesus has moral authority and a capacity for feeling-with, or true empathy, and for suffering-with, or compassion, that could mitigate or alleviate her own pain. Evident too is the fact that she is moving from belief (intellectual knowledge) to faith (relationship, experience). But from what is she suffering?

It becomes immediately apparent that her suffering is vicarious or "sympathetic." She is suffering because her daughter is suffering. She is truly suffering, is physically and emotionally racked, with compassion and empathy. Her pain is her daughter's pain. Her plea is on behalf of a child "tormented by a demon" (v. 22).

This woman represents all people—parents, women, mothers— who are racked by the pain of their children and by their own powerlessness to quell it. She represents all who suffer impotently because of the unimagined and unimaginable suffering of those they love. She represents all who have experienced the pain of others and the numbing pain caused by others. She may have no real idea of what "a demon" actually means, but she knows in every fiber of her being what it is to be tormented, because someone she loves is tormented, and that person's torment is her own. Her predicament cannot fail to touch Jesus, the compassionate one.

"But he did not answer her at all" (v. 23). This is one of the most shocking things ever reported about Jesus. His silence is quite incomprehensible and completely out of character. A high Christology may argue that Jesus was testing the woman and that he knew exactly how he was going to treat her. But a high Christology is quite unconvincing because it would attempt to justify his apparently rather rude behavior. A low Christology, on the other hand, might be very struck by the possibility that Jesus himself was completely taken aback, completely unprepared for this woman's passion. He needed a moment to gather his wits about him, to think, to ponder, and to respond appropriately. He needed time, and he took his time, because something profound was happening. This woman would not be the only one changed by this particular encounter.

The disciples of Jesus were probably just as tired as Jesus was, and even more enervated: they had, after all, just been rescued from a violent storm, and in Peter's case, from drowning. They seem to be at the point of exhaustion, because they plead with Jesus to do something, anything, to satisfy the woman and to give them some respite. But Jesus of course would never resort to cheap miracles or dispense cheap grace. Tired though he may well be, he is about to summon his reserves of energy to address this importunate but generous-spirited woman. Yet when he does finally respond, it is not to offer a solution and not even to offer consolation. His response actually comes across as being rather disrespectful. It has the character of a point-blank refusal, and even borders on an insult: "I was sent only to the lost sheep of the House of Israel" (v. 24). She certainly was "a lost sheep," but she was not "of his flock," not recognizable to the shepherd, and not "of the House of Israel." If what Jesus said was true, then she was excluded and there was simply nothing more to be said.

The starkness of these words and the awfulness of their implication have reverberated down through the ages, leaving commentators looking for loopholes in order to excuse Jesus. Maybe the words just *sound* harsh: it depends upon how they are said. But this is a truly pathetic argument: the words do sound callous, not only to us but to the woman, and surely to those with her in the crowd. So, was Jesus just trying to test the woman's persistence and had already intended to reward her? Again, this is a very weak argument: the woman's humiliation and embarrassment are hard to explain or justify with any argument. Given the broad context of Jesus' own life, is there no other credible explanation? Apparently there is not, unless we take a glimpse at the human Jesus behind the miracle-worker's exterior.

For Jesus, this encounter, perhaps more than any other, seems to offer a moment of insight and enlightenment. There were other people whose deep faith left Jesus nearly at a loss for words: the centurion who felt himself unworthy to have Jesus enter his house; and other women, one suffering from hemorrhaging and another who was determined to anoint him. But this woman was different. She was an outsider and Jesus had ostensibly come for the overlooked insiders, the *lost sheep* of Israel. Or had he? Had he really only come for Israel? Had Jesus not come to be God's all-embracing, inclusive love, to show that God is not partisan and that God will never quench a smoldering wick or reject a broken heart? Had he not declared, in the synagogue at Nazareth that he was the long-awaited fulfillment of Isaiah's promise "to bring good news to the poor...to proclaim release to the captives, and recovery of sight to the blind, to let the oppressed go free"? (Lk 4:18). He had indeed proclaimed the Good News to the poor, liberated people who were captive to illnesses of various kinds, and brought sight to the blind. But was not this woman and, most particularly, the daughter on whose behalf she was begging, was she not among the very downtrodden he had pledged himself to raise up?

Jesus' silence may have been necessary in order to give him time to think, and his response may have been conventional enough. But neither his apparently cold silence nor his seemingly cold answer was ultimately satisfactory to Jesus, and certainly not to the woman. Reflection upon the heart of his mission was about to make him change his mind (something a high Christology is uncomfortable with). The woman may not have the sophistication to argue with him, but she surely had a compassionate heart that resonated with his own. She had not remained at a distance from Jesus and, by this time, was very close to him, kneeling, showing deep respect and vulnerability. She had little to lose and a great deal to gain for her daughter, but she was not going to allow herself to be shamed or humiliated by this man, for she could see through social status and into his compassionate heart. She has eyes of faith. Having first addressed Jesus respectfully as "Lord" (v. 22), she refused to change her mind and again addresses him in the same way, "Lord" (v. 25). With utter simplicity she says only: "Help me" (v. 25).[22] It is profoundly simple, profoundly moving, and profoundly trusting. It cannot fail to move Jesus the compassionate one.

And so it is all the more startling and disturbing that, far from softening towards her, Jesus seems to become even more remote, falling back on another tired old excuse for his unwillingness to help her. He says, "It is not fair to take the children's food and throw it to the [house-]dogs" (v. 26), in what can appear to be quite a heartless response. Many have tried to soften the words and to excuse Jesus, yet when all is said, it seems that Jesus is really struggling here to be faithful to his Abba, without being pitiless towards the woman. And it seems that he is not yet sure of the way forward.

The woman is no philosopher, but she is a mother, and now she sees her chance, now she can seize the initiative, now she will capitalize on her hardheaded practical wisdom and drive home the advantage she perceives from this talk of dogs. She will actually help Jesus understand how his mission must proceed.[23] Quick as a flash, she responds that some dogs ("housedogs" in the Jerusalem Bible) are more tolerated than others, and even have certain domestic privileges. At least the scraps that fall from the table can be claimed by these dogs, and no one is worse off for that. It is a brilliant response, insightful rather than insolent, deferential rather than disrespectful. It seems to make Jesus snap out of his introspectiveness and return to reality—her reality. All his affirmation and compassion are contained in the encouraging words he now speaks: "Woman, great is your faith! Let it be done for you as you wish" (v. 28). She had respectfully called him "Lord." Now he returns the favor and calls her "Woman," a title of considerable respect and intimacy, previously reserved for his mother, for Mary Magdalen, and a very few others.

As we look more closely at this story we may be able to see Jesus struggling with a moral dilemma. We may more readily and sympathetically appreciate how tired and depleted he was. We may be edified by the tenacity of a mother's faith, and be reminded that unlikely people can be the best of teachers. If we are prepared to look for the humanity in Jesus, we may find it in this story and be reminded that even he has something to learn as well as something to teach, something to receive as well as something to give. It's a comforting, and maybe even a surprising, lesson.

Endnotes

19. See also Mark 7:24–30. Again, I follow Matthew's account because there are one or two details that become pertinent as we consider the process of coming to faith.
20. Jesus addressed the woman with a hemorrhage as his "daughter," which would make her also a daughter of Abraham (Mk 5:34). He is even more explicit with the bent-over woman (Lk 13:16).
21. *Rachamim* in Hebrew and *splangkizein* in Greek, the verb "to be compassionate" is associated with the entrails and, more particularly, the womb.
22. The Jerusalem Bible translation has her saying "sir" first (v. 22) and "Lord" second on this occasion (v. 26), indicating a more gradual progression from less to more formal, less faith-filled to more faith-filled.
23. A curious and priceless capacity of a truly interested stranger or outsider is the ability to help insiders come to greater clarity about

the meaning of their own lives. Jesus himself does this for the disciples on the road to Emmaus (Lk 24:32). Here, the Canaanite woman seems to do it for Jesus.

CHAPTER SEVEN

A Father's Faith

(Mk 9:14–29)[24]

(14) *When they came to the disciples,*[25] *they saw a great crowd around them, and some scribes arguing with them.* (15) *When the whole crowd saw him [Jesus], they were immediately overcome with awe, and they ran forward to greet him.* (16) *He asked them, "What are you arguing about with them?"* (17) *Someone from the crowd answered him, "Teacher, I brought you my son; he has a spirit that makes him unable to speak;* (18) *and whenever it seizes him, it dashes him down; and he foams and grinds his teeth and becomes rigid; and I asked your disciples to cast it out, but they could not do so."* (19) *He answered them, "You faithless generation, how much longer must I be among you? How much longer must I put up with you? Bring him to me."* (20) *And they brought the boy to him. When the spirit saw him, immediately it convulsed the boy, and he fell on the ground and rolled about, foaming at the mouth.* (21) *Jesus asked the father, "How long has this been happening to him?" And he said, "From childhood.* (22) *It has often cast him into the fire and into the water, to destroy him; but if you are able to do anything, have pity on us and help us."* (23) *Jesus said to him, "If you are able!—All things can be done for the one who believes."* (24) *Immediately the father of the child cried out, "I believe; help my unbelief!"* (25) *When Jesus saw that a crowd came running together, he rebuked the unclean spirit, saying to it, "You spirit that keep this boy from speaking and hearing, I*

*command you, come out of him, and never enter him again!"
(26) After crying out and convulsing him terribly, it came out, and
the boy was like a corpse, so that most of them said, "He is dead."
(27) But Jesus took him by the hand and lifted him up, and he
was able to stand. (28) When he had entered the house, his disciples
asked him privately, "Why could we not cast it out?" (29) He
said to them, "This kind can come out only through prayer."*

The disciples and perhaps especially the apostles, sometimes appear as foils for Jesus' teaching. In other words, Jesus can call people to faith, he can inform them about the power of faith to change the world, and he can even demonstrate before their very eyes that this power is actually at work, and yet all the time his inner circle of companions remain far from faith, slow-witted, and even obdurate. One of the effects of this is that it can shame, or shake up, the apostles or disciples. Another is that it can encourage or stimulate people in the crowd. But a third effect should be that it influences us modern-day onlookers. Isn't it true that some of us respond better to a challenge when we know that even the "professionals" do not measure up, and when we feel personally encouraged by someone with moral authority? So what can this story of encounter teach us?

This episode starts when the "Big Three"—Peter, James, and John—have just returned from the mountain where they witnessed the Transfiguration. They witnessed, but they did not of course understand. They witnessed, but did not absorb. They witnessed, but did not apply any lesson. As they came down the mountain, Jesus warned them, not for the first time, to keep the experience to themselves and not to tell what they had seen. Mark observes that indeed "they kept the matter to themselves." Another translation (the Jerusalem Bible) says something rather different: "They observed the warning *faithfully*" (9:10). Thus, they did the correct thing, but it is highly unlikely that *faith* had much to do with it, since what they had witnessed does not seem to have made much of an impression upon them: at least not a clear or comprehensible impression. Like these three, we too sometimes do the correct thing almost by accident.

In any event, Peter, James, and John will have had little time to talk about the event, and now their attention is quickly diverted. They are about to join the rest of the disciples when they encounter a commotion that has broken out just ahead of them. A crowd has gathered, and there is a confrontation between some of Jesus' disciples and some of the scribes. The crowd surges forward toward Jesus. But before Jesus can discover what exactly is going on, an unnamed man shouts out. "Teacher," he cries (v. 17). He proceeds to explain that he had brought his son who is suffering from seizures: "He has a spirit that makes him unable to speak" (v. 17). He had already brought him to the disciples in the hope of a cure, but without success.

Jesus responds: "You faithless generation, how much longer must I be among you? How much longer must I put up with you?" (v. 19). Harsh words, these, and words marinated in exasperation. The chosen and preferred disciples were clearly not coming quickly to faith in Jesus (hence "faithless"), and as a direct consequence no deeds of power, or miracles, were occurring. No faith, no miracles. Jesus is evidently deeply disappointed in his chosen ones. Yet he will certainly not use showmanship or superficially spectacular behavior as a way to entice members of the wider community to faith. However, he does focus immediately on the man who calls him teacher. Turning to him, he says: "Bring him [the boy] to me" (v. 19).

Jesus will now teach all the disciples a profound lesson about his mission, by turning to an anonymous and unimportant man and successfully calling him to faith. The man has identified and addressed Jesus as "teacher" [*didascalê*]. He has indicated his intention of bringing his sick son to Jesus for the Master to cast out the demon or mute spirit that was making his life a misery. The disciples had evidently tried to do something on their own, but had only succeeded in embarrassing themselves. So the man appeared somewhat relieved to see Jesus himself approaching.

As soon as the boy comes before Jesus he is convulsed by a seizure: "When the spirit saw him [Jesus], immediately it threw the boy into convulsions, and he fell on the ground and rolled about, foaming at the mouth" (v. 20). It is as if the spirits know they are outclassed

when Jesus is around: they thrash around and convulse their hosts in
complete indecision about whether to opt for fight or flight. The father explains that his son has been afflicted since childhood and provides some details about the illness, describing the effectively lifelong
imprisonment from which Jesus will liberate him. With a degree of
diffidence—not to be confused with lack of faith—the father appeals
to Jesus for help, "If you are able to do anything" (v. 22). Jesus reacts
rather quickly, turning the conditional form into an exclamation: "If
you are able!" he says, amazed: "All things can be done for the one
who believes" (v. 23). (Again, the Jerusalem Bible is more *theologically*
precise, giving us the phrase: "Anyone who has faith.")

With no hesitation at all, the young man's father responds to Jesus'
catechesis with the classic statement: "I believe; help my unbelief!"
(or from the Jerusalem Bible again: "I do have faith. Help the little
faith I have") (v. 24). In one single utterance, he has made both an
explicit act of faith and a request, asking again, but this time more
explicitly, for help. In the first instance he had said, "If you are able,
have pity on us and *help* us" (v. 23), implying that he wanted the help
that would restore his son's health. Now his request for help is much
more specific: he asks for help with his own struggling, fledgling faith
(v. 25). It is this more mature request that impresses Jesus who immediately rewards it by granting the original request. Addressing the cause
of the boy's distress and in the idiom of his culture, Jesus commands
the unclean spirit to leave the boy forever (v. 25).

The instantaneous response of Jesus endorses the father's disposition: from identifying Jesus as "teacher," he moved to requesting help.
The next time he spoke to Jesus it was to make his bold declaration of
faith. Three steps are all he needed to be converted to explicit faith in
Jesus. Since faith is exactly what Jesus is looking for as he proceeds
with his ministry, the reader or listener will sense that the man's faith
will be rewarded in rather spectacular fashion.

No matter who is rendered unfree or victimized, if there is faith
there is always the possibility of healing and freedom. This story illustrates that the faith of one person can also be instrumental: one
person's faith can affect another person's life. Faith can reside within

and animate a community. Bernard Lonergan[26] once remarked that such conversion "can happen to many, and they can form a community to sustain one another in their self-transformation, and to help one another in working out the implications and fulfilling the promise of their new life." This present case seems to be an instance of one man's faith serving the wider community by nurturing that community's own fragile faith. We will see it again later, with the example of a woman's faith (Jn 4). It is worth pondering deeply: dare we believe that our steadfast faith and faithfulness can also have a positive effect on the wider community?

Anyone familiar with stories of spirit possession from another time or place, or with the contemporary folk understanding of the personal causation invoked to account for and explain sickness, will appreciate what happens next. The patient, having been confronted by a powerful and persuasive outside agent, reacts physically in the form of a seizure-like response of great intensity, and that is followed by a complete physical collapse. Those who suffer from epilepsy and experience grand mal seizures, manifest almost exactly the response recorded in Mark's story. The dramatic point is made when the crowds see the almost catatonic figure of the boy, provoking many of the people to state flatly that he is dead. This also provides the literary contrast between (apparent) death and (new) life, and between the boy's former imprisonment or servitude and his present liberation, between the skepticism of the people and the father's faith.

Jesus reaches out and takes the boy by the hand. Here is yet another touching example of his way of encountering people, and also another contrast between the roughness of the evil spirit that was believed to have overtaken the boy and the gentleness of the healing outreach of the Master. But the storyteller adds that not only did Jesus reach out and touch the boy, "he lifted him up" ("raised" in the Jerusalem Bible translation) (v. 27). In the language of miracles, this is resurrection; in more metaphorical terms, it is helping the boy to be upstanding, upright, and able to stand on his own two feet. He is not only restored but is now able to take his rightful place in the ranks of the fully human: the adult world. He is restored to the community, to take his place there and to remind the community itself of the possibility of transformation.

Once again it may seem the disciples were very impressed and willing learners, for they asked Jesus to explain their own inability to bring about such restoration and reintegration into the community. But there are indications that they were actually more interested in technique and status than in faith and service: Jesus tells them somberly that they still have a very long way to go. This kind of healing requires prayer, he tells them. And they have virtually no idea what that might mean.

Prayer bespeaks a relationship with God. Prayer is the raising up of the mind and heart, above narrow self-interest and beyond the horizon of the possible. Prayer is the elevation of the spirit from the mundane to the realm of the Creator. Prayer is the willingness to be led, the hunger to be taught, the deep desire to be inspired by the God who turns people's lives inside out so that they are directed toward others—in particular, the needy and poor people—rather than inverted or limited by the immediate horizon. Prayer is the condition that makes and strengthens faith. Without prayer there is no faith to form the rich soil, the humus, from within which miracles grow. Without faith there can be no miracles of grace.

At the end of this story there are both winners and losers. The unnamed father and his oppressed son are happy and healed. But the disciples, both those fresh from witnessing the Transfiguration and the wider group of disciples and followers, appear to be no wiser and no more faith-filled after this deed of power than before. All we know is that most of the crowd said that the boy was dead, and there were no dissenting voices from the inner group of disciples. The father of the epileptic boy had shown faith and asked for greater faith. The disciples had done neither. They do not seem to be very quick learners.

So Jesus and his disciples continue their progress through Galilee, Jesus cautioning them not to make him into a cult figure but warning them of his impending death, and the disciples failing to understand a word of it, and even afraid to ask what it all could mean.

Endnotes

24. See also Matthew 17:14–21 and Luke 9:37–43.
25. Jesus, Peter, James, and John were coming down from the mountain and the Transfiguration. Now they rejoin the rest of the disciples.
26. Bernard Lonergan, *Method in Theology*. London: Darton, Longman & Todd, 1972: 130–1.

CHAPTER EIGHT

A Bent-Over Woman

(Lk 13:10–17)

(10) *Now he [Jesus] was teaching in one of the synagogues on the sabbath.* (11) *And just then there appeared a woman with a spirit that had crippled her for eighteen years. She was bent over and was quite unable to stand up straight.* (12) *When Jesus saw her, he called her over and said, "Woman, you are set free from your ailment."* (13) *When he laid his hands on her, immediately she stood up straight and began praising God.* (14) *But the leader of the synagogue, indignant because Jesus had cured on the sabbath, kept saying to the crowd, "There are six days on which work ought to be done; come on those days and be cured, and not on the sabbath day."* (15) *But the Lord answered him and said, "You hypocrites! Does not each of you on the sabbath untie his ox or his donkey from the manger, and lead it away to give it water?* (16) *And ought not this woman, a daughter of Abraham whom Satan bound for eighteen long years, be set free from this bondage on the sabbath day?"* (17) *When he said this, all his opponents were put to shame; and the entire crowd was rejoicing at all the wonderful things that he was doing.*

Eighteen years is an awfully long time to be sick. The woman in this story lived at a time when the life expectancy was less than forty years. When it takes twelve or thirteen years to become an adult (a full social person), eighteen years is almost a lifetime. Eighteen years after the beginning of adult life takes a person almost to the end. Time is running out.

The bent-over woman can represent anyone who has been victimized or neglected for a long time. Hers was no ordinary illness. In a society with rudimentary healthcare, she might have coped with ordinary illness. No, this woman was "possessed" by an evil spirit. That is to say, she was oppressed by something evil, and the signs she carried were visible for all to see. Not only was she quite incapable of improving her situation, she was also a pariah, an outcast in the sight of her neighbors and peers. People would want to avoid this manifestation of evil and the kind of people identified with it. This woman was socially dead.

Social death in a small community is no less real than physical death. Social death implies that a person has no status, no social identity. People avoid, or actively shun, those considered socially dead, and a certain kind of theology grows up to support the thinking and behavior of the broader community. This is how it works: the woman is grossly deformed; this must be a punishment for something she— or another person—did; it cannot be rectified; therefore, it is God's will; so we must avoid any contact with her for fear of contamination; that too is God's will. This is a perfectly logical progression, even though the logic itself is perverted or poisoned. But such logic can operate only too effectively in communities whose members consider themselves to be godly people.

The woman in our story has been bent-over for eighteen years. She cannot even see what is happening around her; her perspective on the world is distorted. Not only is she unable to *stand* up, she can hardly even *look* up. Her eyes are permanently downcast because of her deformity.

It is not easy to imagine eighteen years like this, but we can try. Try to think back eighteen years in your own life. Think of the person you were and where you were then. Try to imagine yourself, caught up in a time warp ever since then, unable to lift your head, being downcast, trying everything you know to improve things but to no avail. Just try to imagine your relationship with God during these years.

"One sabbath day, Jesus was teaching in one of the synagogues, and just then there appeared a woman," says Luke. The Jerusalem Bible again picks up an important nuance, saying simply "a woman was there" (Lk 13:10). Like the woman with a hemorrhage (Mk 5:25), she was *there*: despite everything, she had not given up. She is not talking or drawing attention to herself. She is silent, but *she is there*. She has not abandoned God or worship. She still has faith. This day is no different from the previous one and, as far as she is concerned, the following day will be no different from today. Nevertheless, *she is there*.

And Jesus notices her. With absolutely no preamble, the story says: "When Jesus saw her, he called her over and said, 'Woman, you are set free from your ailment'" (v. 12). It happens in a flash, it changes her entire life, and its impact will be felt, not only on the bystanders but even on those who encounter this woman, as Jesus did, but after a gap of two thousand years. The most significant aspect of this encounter is that Jesus assures the woman that she is *cured*: it has already happened. This use of the passive, sometimes called the divine passive, indicates that it is God who has done this thing; and it hardly takes a second for the woman herself to feel the effect. "When he [Jesus] laid his hands on her, immediately she stood up straight" (v. 13). But the healing had actually preceded the laying on of hands. No sooner said than done.

This steadfast, faithful woman does not jump for joy or even think about herself. Her response is to glorify God. How does she do this? No words are recorded, and her soul does not magnify the Lord in so many words. So she must have glorified God in her body, this near-useless body. But no body, and nobody, is utterly useless; no matter how ill, how old, or how disfigured, every body, and every human being, is able to glorify God. So she must have jumped for joy. She is animated now and she must have been quite a spectacle.

In the encounter between Jesus and the woman at the well (Jn 4), Jesus promised "living water" (v. 10) as something "gushing up to eternal life" (v. 14). The verb used there actually means "jumping up," in the way an excited person would. Here, in Luke's story, is an embodiment of this bubbling, effervescent, *new life*. After eighteen years, it is not surprising that she should jump for joy; but it is admirable that her faith should have endured despite everything, until this moment.

Who, then, is this universal woman, and how can her experience provide some insight for our own? Perhaps I too am bent-over, enfeebled, unfree, victimized, unable to stand upright. Some "demons" may come from outside; the demons of violence or other forms of abuse. But some demons come from within; the demons of dependency, low self-esteem, insecurity, or the fear of failure. Whether from within or without, the effect is much the same: the experience of disapproval, rejection, or exclusion. The bent-over woman would have been familiar with all of these effects.

Back now to Jesus. Having healed the woman unconditionally, he next turned his attention to the crowd. But they were not just a crowd. They were, first, the synagogue officials, and then those gathered within the synagogue. They were the believers, the faithful—at least they were the worshipers. But Jesus immediately rounded on them all and called them hypocrites: people hiding behind the mask of respectability; two-faced people who put on a public face that belies their inner state; legalists who have lost, or never had, compassion. These are the people for whom Jesus reserves his most uncompromising judgments. They are the people who should know better. Part of the trouble is precisely that they give the impression that they do know better: better than others, better even than God. These are the most dangerous people because they abuse others. They are no better than the demons believed to possess the bent-over woman.

The official became self-righteously indignant (v. 14), yet was cowardly. The cause of his indignation was Jesus, but rather than stand up to Jesus, he turned on the people. This official gives a completely unnecessary explanation for his irritation (everyone *knew* it was the Sabbath). He wanted to clarify the legal issue in order to catch Jesus in the wrong and justify his own lack of compassion. He actually makes things worse when he says airily, "There are six days on which work ought to be done; come on those days and be cured, and not on the sabbath day" (v. 14)—as if the bent-over woman would have received any more encouragement, much less healing, if she came on a weekday. This is the very kind of self-justification used by people who habitually do not lift a finger for the sake of justice. And it provokes Jesus to his own, godly indignation.

Individuals (in the person of the official) and institutions (in the persons of the worshipers) are collectively hypocrites when they allow the law to bind rather than to set free, when they are complicit in maintaining structures that justify the status quo in the face of palpable injustice, and when they make spurious appeal to God's law while perpetuating enfeeblement and victimization. There is no worse epithet on the lips of Jesus than "hypocrite!"

Jesus does not simply restore this individual bent-over woman, but offers lessons of much wider applicability, lessons we can apply to ourselves. First, he lays hands on her. God, who is also the "Incarnate One," the "True Man," reaches out in the most human way to encounter this misshapen and unlovely woman. She whom people avoided, even with their eyes and certainly with their embraces, was gathered in a healing God-embrace. Every God-embrace restores and heals, encourages and uplifts. She who was shunned by others—others who claimed to be acting in a godly way—was now embraced by the Incarnate One of God in order to unmask the lie that can breed at the heart of every religious system. By setting her free and enabling her to stand upright, Jesus was simultaneously reminding every generation that God is an advocate of victims, not a heartless invigilator or enforcer of the law.

Second, he calls her "daughter of Abraham."[27] This is enormously important, because it emphasizes that her dignity is no less than that of any official or member of the synagogue. As a woman in a patriarchal culture, she is relatively unimportant and expected to contribute to *other people's* families rather than her own: she will be a mother for other men's children rather than a mother for her own. But as a "daughter of Abraham," she is being identified as a legitimate descendant of the patriarch in her own right. She is not only someone's mother or someone's wife (defined functionally), but as the descendant of the prophet she is defined as intrinsically part of the kinship structure of the Chosen People. She is raised up, enhanced, dignified by Jesus and accorded exactly the same status as those "sons of Abraham" who look upon her with such disparagement and antipathy. Jesus is subverting the entire kinship system by calling her a daughter of Abraham. In a patrilineal society (where descent is reckoned only through the direct male line and cannot be transmitted by women) and a patriarchal one (where all authority is exercised explicitly, and only, through males), this is Jesus at his most outrageous and subversive. It is also Jesus the righteous and compassionate one.

But Jesus is not finished: not only does he incorporate her into the kinship system in a way that makes her the equal of any man, he asserts that his act of healing, far from merely being permitted by the spirit if not the letter of the law, was actually *required by it*. For if the effect of the law is to "hold bound" the subjects of the law, then the law is a perversion of justice: God's justice. Therefore, it is *incumbent* on anyone who can see this unjust state of affairs to take whatever steps necessary to rectify it: even on the Sabbath, even for a woman in a man's world.

Third, by espousing the cause of the victimized—whether precisely as a woman, or as one caught by patriarchal injustices, or as someone victimized by the application of Sabbath law—Jesus gives heart to all other bent-over people: the text says that "the entire crowd was rejoicing" (v. 17) at the wonderful things Jesus was doing. Of course they were, because his behavior offered them hope.

What, finally, is the significance of "eighteen years" for you who read this story? Perhaps, it is a reminder of many, many years of being unable to stand up straight because of some form of oppression or victimization. Perhaps, it is a reminder of your enduring faithfulness, of your still *being there*, in spite of all the difficulties and the long, long years. Perhaps, it is a timely reminder that you must not lose faith, and with God's help, you will not lose faith—even though the pain sometimes seems unbearable and never-ending.

Certainly, there are far too many bent-over women in today's church. And there are some bent-over men as well. They are bent-over by the law and its application, by theology and clericalism, by patriarchy and hypocrisy, by a lack of accountability and an obscene abuse of power. *This is not the will of God.* God's will is that everyone should be able to stand up, upright, and morally straight. God's justice demands that everyone be treated as free, equal people, able to give glory to God. Tragically, after millennia, there are still people who fail to understand that the Sabbath was made for people and that the law is not life. This story reminds us that God is faithful. God wants to enable us to live uprightly, even after eighteen years. Even in old age.

Endnotes

27. This is even more emphatic than calling her simply "daughter." We saw, in the case of the hemorrhaging woman, that Jesus does this. Here, he is quite explicit: she is a daughter of Abraham.

CHAPTER NINE

Ten-Percent Response

(Lk 17:11–19)

(11) *On the way to Jerusalem Jesus was going through the region between Samaria and Galilee.* (12) *As he entered a village, ten lepers approached him. Keeping their distance,* (13) *they called out, saying, "Jesus, Master, have mercy on us!"* (14) *When he saw them, he said to them, "Go and show yourselves to the priests." And as they went, they were made clean.* (15) *Then one of them, when he saw that he was healed, turned back, praising God with a loud voice.* (16) *He prostrated himself at Jesus' feet and thanked him. And he was a Samaritan.* (17) *Then Jesus asked, "Were not ten made clean? But the other nine, where are they?* (18) *Was none of them found to return and give praise to God except this foreigner?"* (19) *Then he said to him, "Get up and go on your way; your faith has made you well."*

Jesus was journeying south, from Galilee to Jerusalem, and was approaching Samaria. He was in the borderlands. We have already seen a number of occasions when his pastoral ministry flourished and his social encounters multiplied when he was boundary-crossing, or betwixt and between. By now we may be on the lookout for significant things to happen on the margins or with socially marginal people. The present occasion brings both geographical margins and socially marginalized people together.

The passage begins with the observation that Jesus was "on the way" (v. 1). This indeed typifies his whole ministry. But in this case, he is explicitly on the way to Jerusalem, on the way to destiny. Yet he is not so preoccupied as to be insensitive to the needy and forgotten. As a kind of effective literary conceit, Luke concludes this particular story by repeating the image: Jesus, himself on the way, will soon meet his death and will therefore need witnesses to continue his work and remain committed to the way. He sends the healed leper *on his way*, but by the time the story has been told, the leper is going a different way altogether from the way he had previously been going.

Jesus, then, enters an unnamed village, metaphorically in the middle of nowhere. He is approached by ten nameless lepers, metaphorically nobodies themselves. The setting could be anywhere and the people could be anyone: here is a good opportunity to apply the lesson to our own situation and our own selves, wherever and whoever we may be.

We are not specifically told that the lepers were all men; they may well have been a mixed group, clinging together for support in a hostile world, much as homeless people do in our big cities today. And we are not specifically told about their disease, for "leprosy" was a very broad term that covered a wide range of skin conditions, from psoriasis to eczema and alopecia to vitiligo, ranging across the dermatological spectrum to include the most virulent forms of Hansen's disease, or leprosy as we commonly know it. What they had in common was some symptom, out of many possible symptoms, that was deemed to make people ritually unclean, to cause them to be prohibited from Temple or synagogue and therefore excluded from religious practice and membership. These "lepers" were social outcasts, and they were as socially dead as the man in the graveyard (Mk 5:2) or the woman with a hemorrhage (Mk 5:25).

This is the only version we have of this particular story, and it is significant that it comes from Luke the physician. Luke was particularly sensitive both to physical and mental ailments, as well as to the universality of Jesus' message. In this story we find Jesus addressing one of the most feared of diseases (full-blown leprosy was, until very recently, thought to be highly and universally contagious; it is not). We see him dealing with a group of people rather than simply with an individual. And we hear him reminding anyone who cares to notice, that geographical boundaries and rules of ritual pollution are not enough to exclude people from God's embrace. There are times in our own lives when we particularly need to be reminded of this point.

The ten pariahs are ambivalent: they both approach Jesus and keep their distance (v. 12). They seem to sense that they must not come too close, for religious and practical reasons, but that this may be the best chance they will ever have for a change of fortune, for survival. Evidently already the reputation of Jesus has gone before him, and it would not have gone unnoticed that he seemed to express a preference for the poorest, the most abject, and the most alienated in society. These lepers surely qualified on all counts. Their call is a familiar one: "Jesus, Master, have mercy on us!" (v. 13). They know his name, they know that he is a man of standing [*epistates* meaning "one who stands over"; "master"], and they believe him to be an agent of God's mercy. That is a very good start.

At times Jesus had been known to say nothing as with the Canaanite woman (Mt 15:23). Or he might ask, "What do you want me to do for you?" as he did to of Bartimaeus (Mk 10:51). Or, he touches or lays hands on people as with the blind man (Jn 9). This occasion is different: immediately Jesus responds by saying, "Go and show yourselves to the priests" (v. 14). The "go" is not yet a commission, nor does Jesus tell them to "come" when they have completed his instructions. He simply sends them to the religious authorities, without elaboration.

In that time and culture, there were few possibilities open to a person who was excluded from public worship by virtue of sin or sickness. Assuming that a sinner repented and made the appropriate offering, it might be possible to be reinstated. And if a physical condition should change (we may think of Mary and Joseph going to be presented in the Temple, in Lk 2:22–25), certain appropriate rites of purification might be performed. But many people who had been categorized as sinners were effectively prohibited from making either restitution or a religious offering, since their money was contaminated (by earnings from prostitution or income gained through extortionate collecting of taxes). Another heavy restriction was related to people such as lepers: once they were given a certificate that identified what was seen as a chronic and incurable condition, there was no way it could be revoked, except if the priests were to see with their own eyes that a person or persons were evidently free from any ailment, and perform a ritual purification.[28] So Jesus bids the ten sick people to "show themselves"—literally—to the priests. He is not simply planning some private cure, but also making a public statement.

Poor people and sick people are often overlooked or forever pushed around, sent here and there with vague promises of redress or assistance. Theirs is a never-ending round of deferrals and dead-ends. They become used to excuses or prevarication from bureaucrats or people without compassion. We have to wonder what these ten lepers must have felt when Jesus appeared to dismiss them and send them on their way without really having encountered them. Did they set off with a spring in their step, or simply accept another rebuff, and go their way with no intention of heading for the priests? We cannot know, but we can imagine. And we can imagine their excitement when, "as they went, they were made clean" (v. 14). Wherever they were actually going, they had kept together. That was probably necessary. If they had dispersed and made their way alone, they might not have noticed any immediate change.

People ravaged by true leprosy lose all tactile sensation: the skin becomes desensitized. Then the skin, and the bone beneath it, begins to atrophy and die. The fact that the ten stuck together was certainly for the best. Now perhaps one of them observed that another's limp was gone; perhaps someone suddenly noticed a smile where previously there had only been a paralyzed face. Maybe one or another of them gradually became convinced that feeling had returned to a long-dead limb or that a quick inventory confirmed that a lost digit had reappeared. It must have been very exciting. But together they could affirm and confirm their amazing good fortune. Of course, we can never know, but we can imagine.

We can imagine incredulity and excitement, laughter and relief. We can imagine emotion so great that they never did get to show themselves to the priests because all they could think about was the moment and the ecstasy. All self-consciousness had vanished, and all shame had evaporated: all they wanted to do was strip naked and look at themselves, indeed show themselves to *everybody*. Anyone who has seen any medical cures in some of the world's poorest countries, will be familiar with the level of excitement generated by totally unexpected restoration to health. No wonder the ten did not show themselves to the priests. No wonder that nine of them did not even think about Jesus, at least not immediately. The wonder is that even one had the presence of mind to make the connection, to stop in his tracks, to think for a moment, and to return. Perhaps he was more introspective; perhaps he was a man of faith.

In his moment of elation, this man shouted out in a loud voice, and the praise of God was on his lips. This nameless man does indeed show signs of faith. He shows that not only has he been cured but that he has been truly healed. A cure represents a reversal of some physical condition and a restoration to physical health, but a healing represents a different level of response. Healing takes place at the metaphysical level, at the level of the soul, at a level too deep for words. Healing is God's shalom, acknowledged by the human awareness of having received something far beyond the physical.[29] According to Luke's story, all ten lepers were cured of their condition. According to Luke's story too, only one was also truly healed: restored to a full relationship with God through both divine initiative and human response.

This restoration is exemplified in the posture of the healed man: he "prostrated himself at the feet of Jesus and thanked him" (v. 16). There is no explicit act of faith, no identification of Jesus as "Son of God," "Messiah," or any other title. But there is a giving of thanks, thanksgiving (the text says *eukaristōn,* a participle form meaning "thanking [him]"). Here is a humble eucharistic act, a simple sacrament of gratitude to the healer. And the evangelist notes pointedly, "He was a Samaritan" (v. 16). Not only did no Israelite return to give thanks, but Jesus acknowledged that the thanks of a Samaritan was entirely acceptable and appropriate. Luke is pushing the horizons of his listeners and readers, showing that God is not without witnesses in unlikely places.

Jesus finishes by making a point. But the point seems as much to favor and endorse "this foreigner" (v. 18) as to lament the ungraciousness of those who might have been expected to be more forthcoming in their gratitude. Foreigners can indeed give glory to God. Marginalized people, and society's nobodies, may be out of sight but they are not out of mind: not where Jesus is concerned. If we can imagine the understandable joy of the other nine, perhaps we should not see this as a story of ingratitude as much as a story of God's gratuitous grace, available to the most unlikely, and sometimes acknowledged by the most unlikely among them, because the end of the story does not concern the nine, but focuses on the tenth, the minority, the not-to-be-overlooked remnant, the ten percent.

Jesus finally addresses this single representative individual, the one who resisted the pressure of his group and perhaps lost the support of his group forever, but who discovered an undreamed-of new relationship and a new possibility. No longer does this man need the relative security of the group of ten. Now he is rehabilitated. Now he is restored. Now he is deeply healed. This man will always be called to live in some kind of community, but in the future it will not be a community of nobodies or a community of outsiders. Now the nobody has become somebody, the outsider has become an insider, the aimless person has an aim in life. Having called him to health and healing, Jesus now sends and commissions this man to be a healed healer himself: "Get up, and go on your way; your faith has made you well" (v. 19). But since it is faith that brought him to this miracle of healing, it will be faith that brings him home in the end. And since Jesus has bidden him to "get up," he has become empowered as an upright citizen and a person of restored integrity. This transformation, together with his newfound faith, will ensure that when he goes on his way, it is also the way of the one who is himself the Way, the Truth, and the Life. And if that is the case, then he will surely encounter other nobodies in his turn.

May we who absorb this story and stories like it, count our own blessings, give thanks to God, and go on our way—God's way—to glorify the God who restores us, and to reach out to those who still do not understand their own worth.

Endnotes

28. There is an excellent summary, easily available, in *Encyclopedia Britannica* [15th ed], 15:303.
29. We noted this in the story of the paralyzed man (Ch. 1 above).

CHAPTER TEN

A Poor Rich Man

(Mk 10:17–22)

(17) *As he [Jesus] was setting out on a journey, a man ran up and knelt before him, and asked him, "Good Teacher, what must I do to inherit eternal life?"* (18) *Jesus said to him, "Why do you call me good? No one is good but God alone.* (19) *You know the commandments: 'You shall not murder; You shall not commit adultery; You shall not steal; You shall not bear false witness; You shall not defraud; Honor you father and mother.'"* (20) *He said to him, "Teacher, I have kept all these since my youth."* (21) *Jesus, looking at him, loved him and said, "You lack one thing; go, sell what you own, and give the money to the poor, and you will have treasure in heaven; then come, follow me."* (22) *When he heard this, he was shocked and went away grieving, for he had many possessions.*

There is a fundamental difference between taking an initiative and responding to a call. In the first case the movement starts from within: the individual is the initiator. In the second case it starts outside the individual: another person is the initiator. In the life and ministry of Jesus, those who take initiatives do not always become disciples.

Typically, Jesus invites people to respond to his call. Of course, he may use someone's initiative and redirect or purify it in such a way that Jesus himself becomes both the real source of the call and the real source of the subsequent commission: "come" precedes "go"; being called is prior to being sent. Nevertheless, initiatives alone are not indicators of discipleship.

In what is now chapter 10 of Mark's Gospel, we are given two extraordinary, contrasting, and very familiar stories. However, each may contain certain overlooked yet significant details. The first may be understood as an ultimately failed initiative, and the second as a successful response to a call. The evangelist places the "bookends" strategically, emphasizing and contrasting these two wonderful vignettes. The first, of course, is the story we know as "The rich (young) man," and the second is the story of blind Bartimaeus.

Jesus is once again "setting out on his journey," when suddenly a man comes out of nowhere and, in a gesture of homage, throws himself at his feet. We are not told much about the man: neither his name nor his age. We may think of him as being young, perhaps because of this introductory gymnastic gesture. It is certainly one effective way of stopping a person in his tracks and, in this case it appears to work: the man has Jesus' undivided attention. For his part, he is focused and rather intense for he immediately blurts out, "Good Teacher, what must I do to inherit eternal life?" (v. 17). Not only must he have known Jesus therefore by contact or repute (for he identifies him by the formal title of "teacher"), but he evidently expects some kind of immediate answer to what is actually a foundational and highly controversial question. Even more promising: the very urgency of his demeanor gives every indication of his willingness to follow the teacher's instructions implicitly and without question. Nevertheless, it is instructive to note that this man is seeking help with a theological point, unlike most other people, who have something much more immediate in mind. They come explicitly for healing and for liberation, either for themselves or for others.

Jesus, of course, has plenty of experience of being bombarded with requests for healing, but requests for information or advice are very unusual. Despite his helter-skelter approach, the questioner seems reflective rather than impulsive, and in search of something more than just a "quick fix." His agenda is clear, his approach direct, and his intentions are honorable.

It is easy for a well-intentioned person to be caught off guard by an unexpected request. In his encounters, Jesus sometimes takes the initiative and asks a question: "What do you want me to do?" or "Has no one condemned you?" But in this particular case the request is direct, unequivocal, surprising—and, in these circumstances, somewhat unexpected. Despite all of this, Jesus will not be caught off guard, for he knows very well that he is no purveyor of what Dietrich Bonhoeffer called "cheap grace." This (young) man will find life rather more complicated than he expects. Yet, if he has the capacity for trust, he will also discover the meaning his life so desperately needs and that his heart so deeply desires.

The general orientation of the life and ministry of Jesus might be described as open, or open-ended. Even as this particular encounter takes place, Jesus is setting out on a journey. That could be a metaphor for his whole life: outreach and boundary-breaking are characteristic of his life's work, just as centrifugal movement marks his steps. Moreover, this is a measure not only of his itinerant ministry but of his attitude towards God: his posture is one of openness and availability. Consequently, the question put to him, though disarmingly simple, will immediately evoke a response. But in this particular case it is a response the questioner neither expects nor is able to handle.

Before addressing the question directly however, Jesus addresses the man himself, the person at his feet: a simple but effective sign of good manners and respect. Jesus has been addressed as "good Teacher." Is this also a sign of good manners and respect on the questioner's part, or perhaps an attempt at flattery? Perhaps it is just a superficial identification of the one whom listeners of this story would have come to know as Lord and Savior. Jesus asks for clarification, gently drawing the man to commit himself. "Why do you call me good? No one is good but God alone" (v. 18). Will the man follow Jesus' implicit line of thought and come to faith? Strangely, perhaps, Jesus does not even give him a chance to ponder the question. Perhaps the question was rhetorical. Perhaps the Teacher has a lesson.

The questioner is looking for clarity, and for a response that stipulates a task or program. Not unreasonably one might think, this man wants an answer to his rather specific and calculated question. But Jesus does not always provide clarity, rarely stipulates a task or program, and refuses to set limits to love. Jesus never answers closed questions. Jesus looks for generous and open-ended commitment, not contract workers or laborers who work to rule. He has come to expand imaginations, not to play a political game or be limited to the art of the possible. His agenda is as open as God's love, and his perspective is as wide as God's realm.

So Jesus responds, in a disarmingly simple way, yet surely not as the man imagined. "You know the commandments," he says (v. 19), gently affirming the man's religious knowledge; and he proceeds to catalog those commandments that relate to family and neighbor. But, oddly perhaps, Jesus omits all the commandments directly related to the worship of God. What could be the significance of this?

Perhaps, this man's religious instincts are founded on a sure footing. Certainly, he has a strong social conscience, and he now asserts it by stating quite simply that he has observed all these commandments from his youth (v. 20). How long has that been? If he really is a young man, perhaps he has not kept them long enough to be tested over the long haul. But, perhaps he has: perhaps he has indeed borne the heat and burden of the day. Perhaps he is a true disciple-in-the-making. In any event, the story continues with a very delicate observation: "Jesus, looking at him, loved him" (v. 21). There is something very touching about this picture, and something very attractive about the encounter up to this point.

But Jesus has evidently *not* forgotten the commandments he omitted from his list, for he now asserts unequivocally, incisively: "You lack one thing" (v. 21). Only one! What an amazing affirmation by the teacher. If the pupil now has the courage of his convictions, he will be both gratified by the teacher's approval and anxious to complete his own education. Then, with as little hesitation as the man himself had shown initially, Jesus follows home his point: "Go!"

Jesus is never one to ask the impossible, only the unlikely and unimagined. In the present case, the full significance of his words needs to be understood, for this is neither a simple "go" nor the breathtaking non sequitur or disjunctive command it may appear to be. On the contrary, Jesus' instructions are intended not to produce rupture but to create connection, collaboration, and community. His "go" will be followed by a "come, follow me!" (v. 22). In this way, the man's initiative will have been harnessed as a means of his own discipleship, but it will also have been transformed into a covenant or bond between master and disciple. But that imperative, that command, will also require the man to engage in some very radical and public behavior, and not just privatized piety. This requirement is worth a second look.

With Jesus, "come" and "go" very often occur together: he calls (come) and sends (go) in a single movement. But he almost never sends without first calling a person explicitly.[30] In the present case however the young man had not actually been called, but had taken a commendable initiative—not to say quite a risk—in accosting Jesus. So now Jesus will call him, but in a reversal of the movement he usually employs. The man is first told to "go," and then to "come, follow me." Perhaps, if Jesus had first said "come" and then "go," the man would have been able to manage. But that, after all, appeared unnecessary: the man had already come to Jesus. Yet the prospect of having to go, to sell all he had, and give the money to the poor (v. 21) was evidently just too radical to contemplate. True, Jesus promised treasure in heaven (did that smack too much of "pie in the sky when you die"?); and it is true that he issued the invitation: "Come, follow me," which was an assurance and guarantee that might have been sufficient for other people. But the man was caught off guard, just as he had caught Jesus off guard. And he simply could not cope. Jean Vanier once said that he thought of "the poor" as anyone who can cope—or better, admits it. Theirs is the kingdom of God, but only if they know they can't cope. Perhaps, this young man lacked that self-knowledge, and the willingness to turn to one who could cope.

"At that saying" ("When he heard this" [v.22 in the NRSV translation]), says the storyteller, the man's face fell and he went away as swiftly as he had come. But now sorrow had replaced enthusiasm, and his "great possessions" were insufficient to give him consolation. In good faith, he had sought a reasonable answer to a reasonable, but complex, question. But he had not received an answer: at least, not a simple, reasonable answer. Jesus effectively removes all the limits that hedge this question, identifying the question itself as invalid. Quite simply, there is no single thing that one must do, or can do, to inherit eternal life. No single act will do, for that would be too mechanical, too much like magic. Eternal life is a gift, freely offered to all, yet quite beyond price. We cannot purchase what is priceless, yet if it is freely offered we may accept it wholeheartedly. And if we truly want something that is priceless, we will be prepared to pay any price, prepared to give everything we have. Nothing less than a wholehearted commitment is a legitimate response to God's gift of life. As a result, the man, loved by Jesus, departs, sorrowfully.

This is a stark, sad story: such good intentions, such an unsatisfactory ending. Maybe this was indeed a young man, perhaps even a callow man. But maybe he was also young enough for second thoughts and a second approach to Jesus at a later date. We can only speculate. But we can also draw some conclusions and applications for our own life story.

Not one of us, alone, can generate sufficient commitment to go to others. Discipleship is simply too demanding. First then we must come to Jesus, not once but repeatedly. And however much respect we may have for Jesus as Teacher—even "Good Teacher"—that too is insufficient to sustain what must be a faith commitment for the long haul. Such a commitment will deepen our belief that to "go, sell what you own, and give the money to the poor" (v. 21) is consistent with a developing relationship with Jesus, capable of producing appropriate "treasure in heaven," and consistent with the deepening of our own personal identity. Before we can "go" in this fashion, we must already have come to Jesus. But as we go, we must frequently "come" to Jesus, lest we be burned up, and burned out, by the demands of the poor.

Jesus says: "Follow me." He says: "Give to the poor." He is inviting people to discipleship, and discipleship requires new kinds of relationships, new kinds of community. Rugged individualism is simply not adequate. *Mutual indebtedness* is to be the sign of the Jesus community (see Acts 2:42–47). The rich (young) man is unable to contemplate that concept. He is no less bound than the man living in the tombs, or the community that has become codependent upon him. He is no less bound than the woman with a hemorrhage, or the one bent-over for eighteen years. He is a cautionary example for us, offering us an opportunity to examine ourselves and identify what binds us, what keeps us in chains, bent-over and unfree.

Many of us can, at the very least, imagine undertaking a clearly defined task. But Jesus' refusal to provide closed answers to life's fundamental questions can be infuriating to linear thinkers and rational souls. Yet the pursuit of the realm of God cannot be reduced to a rational or linear agenda. The very question, "What must I do to inherit eternal life?" (v. 17) therefore, is fundamentally flawed: there can be no fixed, closed, programmatic answer. The only answer is the one Jesus gives: "Come, follow me." It demands imagination, vision, and total commitment. It demands trust in the enabling grace of the one who calls. And even though a person brings what they have—good intentions, skills, time, health, enthusiasm, and the rest—there is only truly one thing necessary: everything we are. Or, as T. S. Eliot said so well, "a condition of complete simplicity (*costing not less than everything*)."[31]

Endnotes

30. A notable exception is the case of the man born blind (Jn 9:7), as well as the ten lepers (Lk 17:14).
31. T. S. Eliot, "Little Gidding," Pt. 5.

CHAPTER ELEVEN

"Let Me See Again!"

(Mk 10:46–52)

(46) *They came to Jericho. As he [Jesus] and his disciples and a large crowd were leaving Jericho, Bartimaeus son of Timaeus, a blind beggar, was sitting by the roadside.* (47) *When he heard that it was Jesus of Nazareth, he began to shout out and say, "Jesus, Son of David, have mercy on me!"* (48) *Many sternly ordered him to be quiet, but he cried out even more loudly, "Son of David, have mercy on me!"* (49) *Jesus stood still and said, "Call him here." And they called the blind man, saying to him, "Take heart; get up, he is calling you."* (50) *So throwing off his cloak, he sprang up and came to Jesus.* (51) *Then Jesus said to him, "What do you want me to do for you?" The blind man said to him, "My teacher, let me see again."* (52) *Jesus said to him, "Go; your faith has made you well." Immediately he regained his sight and followed him on the way.*

The rich young man (Mk 10:17–22) was anonymous, and dramatically so. We do not know where he came from ("a man ran up") and we do not know where he went ("he went away, sorrowful"). He might stand for *Everyman.* But the tenth chapter of Mark's Gospel ends with a story about another man, and we know much more about him. We know his name (Bartimaeus). We know something about his origins (blindness, but not from birth, so he has some memory of what sight is and what it means; years of begging). And we can certainly infer something about his subsequent life. The evangelist has beautifully juxtaposed these two stories, and in reading each, we should be conscious of the other.

The storyteller states that Jesus was still "on the way." So often when these words are used they serve as both a literary device to string various incidents together, and as a reminder that Jesus was an itinerant preacher: that was the shape and form his ministry took. He arrived in Jericho, but we are told nothing about what he did there. But as he was leaving the city, there was a blind beggar already "sitting by the roadside" (v. 46). The context and the association of ideas here are interesting: Jesus, who identified himself as *The Way* and called people to come to him to find their way and follow *The Way;* and a blind beggar, already there, already by the wayside, all ready for an encounter with Jesus.

This man comes vividly to life, perhaps because we are given his name and social context: he is "the son of Timaeus" (v. 46), thus Bar-Timaeus. We recall that Simon the Rock, who came to be called Peter, was the son of Jonah, and that Jesus dignified him not only by citing his pedigree ("blessed are you Simon Bar Jonah") but by actually giving him a new name. The same thing happened to Abram after his call, and to Saul after his experience on the Damascus road. A new name signifies a new identity. Thus, naming is very important. We have already noted that Jesus asked the name of the spirits who identified themselves as "Legion" (Mk 5:9). To name someone else indicates authority or power over that person. To name the world itself is likewise to exercise a degree of power. To be named, or to have a name is to be identified, to be given an identity, and placed in a relationship. The young man who went away sad was not identified by name, but Bartimaeus most certainly was. Yet the storyteller does more for us: he gives us both the name of the beggar and the name of his healer: "Jesus of Nazareth" (v. 47), like "Bar-Timaeus," brings intentional and instructive detail to the story. People who are in a relationship need to call one another by name.

Bartimaeus was sitting by the roadside. It would have been exceedingly difficult for a blind beggar to make himself known in a noisy, pressing crowd. But as soon as he "heard that it was Jesus of Nazareth" who had drawn the crowd, "he began to shout" (v. 47). Even before the encounter with Jesus, and long before his actual healing and commissioning, we begin to sense that here is a good and honest man. Jesus often appealed to those with ears, calling them to listen, to hear his word, and to respond to it. Bartimaeus was certainly doing that. We may recall that in ancient Israel one of the defining characteristics of a human being was precisely this—someone with ears to hear, to assimilate, and to respond in a responsible and interactive way. But many people simply failed to act like responsible adults, and many fail to do so even today: physically they have ears yet they do not hear. Jesus frequently chastises people for this all too human failing.

In the eyes of some, a blind beggar like Bartimaeus is less than human. But this blind beggar gives the lie to that opinion because he *heard* and he *responded*. He responded in the very best way he could under these circumstances: he shouted at the top of his voice. He was, after all, separated from Jesus by the milling crowds, and he could not see Jesus because he was blind. But when he *heard* Jesus—or heard that Jesus was very near—he made absolutely sure that Jesus could hear him. If having ears, hearing, assimilating, and responding were criteria of humanness, then Jesus, who had invoked those criteria so often, must surely exemplify them himself. Bartimaeus's instincts, or his growing faith, were strong and sure: so he shouted loud enough to be heard by Jesus as he passed.

And what a shout, and what a voice, and what a plea. "Jesus, Son of David, have mercy on me!" he cried (v. 47). This was no pitiful cry for help, but a bold and assertive act of naming and identification. Nor was this a conventional form of address: Bartimaeus did not simply shout "sir" or "teacher," which would have been respectful but rather general. No, this blind beggar had the boldness—or the familiarity—to use the first name of Jesus, as well as the name that identified his origin: "of Nazareth." Was Jesus becoming like a modern celebrity whose name was public property? Perhaps it was simply that Bartimaeus knew one thing for sure: that this was a once-in-a-lifetime chance. But only if he managed to stop Jesus in his tracks could there be any hope of an encounter or a cure.

If ever we are in a crowd and someone shouts our name, it is virtually impossible not to react instinctively, even though the one who shouts may not actually be addressing us, but another person with the same name as us. Bartimaeus must have known this. If he shouted the name Jesus, Jesus could hardly have stopped himself from reacting; he would surely react and respond. Yet words could also seem overfamiliar or even rude: Bartimaeus was taking liberties with the name of Jesus. Normally, the process is that we first give our name before it can be taken or used by another. To have a stranger call us by our first name is inappropriate. We have no evidence that Jesus had introduced himself or given his name to Bartimaeus. But perhaps he had....

There is much more to come: not only does Bartimaeus claim access to the name of Jesus, but he addresses him as "Son of David" (v. 48). At the very least, this is a messianic title. At the very least, Bartimaeus is publicly acknowledging that he regards Jesus not simply as special, but in some sense as an explicitly godly person. Perhaps his words indicate a good deal more; that he is on his way to faith in the one who passes by.

At this point, the disciples—like self-appointed bodyguards— "sternly ordered him to be quiet" ("scolded him" says the Jerusalem Bible) (v. 48). In a previous story, Mark had told us of the crowds pressing around Jesus (Mk 5:31), and the woman with a hemorrhage who managed to touch him. Perhaps the people—the "in crowd," the disciples—were a little jealous of Jesus-as-celebrity. Perhaps they were just throwing their weight around a little. In any case, Jesus was not impressed by this bullying and attempted a bit of crowd control: he stopped at the sound of Bartimaeus's voice and said, "Call him here" (v. 49). Now we see how fickle these disciples are: in an instant, their attitude changes and their words become gently encouraging, perhaps even sycophantic, as they call the man and curry favor with Jesus: "Take heart; get up, he is calling you" (v. 49). And presumably, they attempt to make some room in the crowd so that Bartimaeus can get through.

We need to imagine the scene: a bustling, noisy throng, a very brief opportunity, and a do-or-die situation; Bartimaeus, excited, apprehensive, and blind. He is close to Jesus, but exactly how close is he? He is not absolutely sure himself. He must move ahead before the crowd closes in around him and his opportunity is lost forever. Absolutely the worst thing to do would be to jump up, trip, and fall flat on his face, not because it would be embarrassing but because he would miss the opportunity of a lifetime. At all costs, he must succeed in this effort to get to Jesus. The only thing—literally the only thing—between him and his hope is his cloak.

The Book of Exodus tells us: "If you take your neighbor's cloak in pawn, you shall restore it before the sun goes down; for it may be your neighbor's only clothing to use as cover; in what else shall that person sleep?" (Ex 22:26–27). But for Bartimaeus, at this moment, there is no other choice: the cloak must go. "So, throwing off his cloak, he sprang up and came to Jesus" (v. 50). What does it matter if he is naked? He is blind, and he neither sees nor cares about other people's reactions. It is a bizarre scene: a naked, or nearly naked, blind beggar standing before Jesus, and a hushed and expectant crowd.

Jesus speaks: he does not call out nor shout, so Bartimaeus had indeed reached his target. The words are gentle and urgent, and very, very close: "What do you want *me* to do for *you*?" (v. 51). It is a doubly important question: beggars usually want alms; is Jesus to be almsgiver today? Does Bartimaeus want money? More important, Jesus will not jump to conclusions or work miracles just for effect: Bartimaeus must state his deepest need and articulate his own desire. Some beggars might well have asked for alms; they would have been used to begging and probably quite unskilled. How would a sighted but totally unskilled man earn a living after a lifetime of begging? Perhaps it would be prudent simply to ask for alms, for almsgiving was one of the most important religious acts: a "good work" that Jesus could hardly fail to honor.

Similarly, some of us may be more comfortable working within our limitations than ready to be extended or challenged, more willing to ask for what we can cope with than to ask for what God might want to give us, more willing to stay in control than to let God into our lives.

But conversion is a fundamental turning around of one's life, and Bartimaeus was about to experience a very dramatic conversion moment. Clearly, and with deep respect, he replied, "My Teacher ("Rabboni" in the Jerusalem Bible), let me see again" (v. 51). There is a poignant urgency in Bartimaeus's words, which are more like "Allow me to see *again*" or "If only I could see *again.*" He remembers the time he could see; he wants it to happen again. He was not always blind, and he might have had hope, once upon a time. There is a rich irony here of course: even before his sight is restored, Bartimaeus already "sees" much more clearly and perceptively than the disciples do.

"Go," says Jesus, "your faith has made you well." And *immediately* his sight returned (v. 52). Again, we see Mark's fondness for this word "immediately": the faith of Bartimaeus, identified by Jesus, is the trigger for his cure. As soon as there is faith, there is an instantaneous miracle. Faith indeed makes miracles. Immediately.

This powerful story has a powerful ending: Bartimaeus followed Jesus along the road. Here is a man who started at the side of the road, on the edge, at the margin, not quite "on track." And what does he do when his sight was restored? He does not run off to start a life for himself. He does not even jump for joy and consider his good fortune. Instead, he moves from the edge of the road to the road itself and follows Jesus, who is himself *The Way.* Bartimaeus is a true disciple, a wayfarer, not going his own way but "on the way" with Jesus, following Jesus on the way. Later, after the Resurrection, Jesus' followers came to be called people of *The Way.* Bartimaeus is a splendid example of that faithfulness. He is a memorable lesson for us all.

CHAPTER TWELVE

Blind Faith

(Jn 9:1–41)

(1) *As he [Jesus] walked along, he saw a man blind from birth.*
(2) *His disciples asked him, "Rabbi, who sinned, this man or his parents, that he was born blind?"* (3) *Jesus answered, "Neither this man nor his parents sinned; he was born blind so that God's works might be revealed in him.* (4) *We must work the works of him who sent me while it is day; night is coming when no one can work.* (5) *As long as I am in the world, I am the light of the world."* (6) *When he had said this, he spat on the ground and made mud with the saliva and spread the mud on the man's eyes,* (7) *saying to him, "Go, wash in the pool of Siloam" (which means Sent). Then he went and washed and came back able to see.* (8) *The neighbors and those who had seen him before as a beggar began to ask, "Is this not the man who used to sit and beg?"* (9) *Some were saying, "It is he." Others were saying, "No, but it is someone like him." He kept saying, "I am the man."* (10) *But they kept asking him, "Then how were your eyes opened?"* (11) *He answered, "The man called Jesus made mud, spread it on my eyes, and said to me, 'Go to Siloam and wash.' Then I went and washed and received my sight."* (12) *They said to him, "Where is he?" He said, "I do not know."*

(13) *They brought to the Pharisees the man who had formerly been blind.* (14) *Now it was a sabbath day when Jesus made the mud and opened his eyes.* (15) *Then the Pharisees also began to ask him how he had received his sight. He said to them,*

"He put mud on my eyes. Then I washed, and now I see."
(16) *Some of the Pharisees said, "This man is not from God, for he does not observe the sabbath." But others said, "How can a man who is a sinner perform such signs?" And they were divided.* (17) *So they said again to the blind man, "What do you say about him? It was your eyes he opened." He said, "He is a prophet."*

(18) *The Jews did not believe that he had been blind and had received his sight until they called the parents of the man who had received his sight* (19) *and asked them, "Is this your son, who you say was born blind? How then does he now see?"* (20) *His parents answered, "We know that this is our son, and that he was born blind;* (21) *but we do not know how it is that now he sees, nor do we know who opened his eyes. Ask him; he is of age. He will speak for himself."* (22) *His parents said this because they were afraid of the Jews; for the Jews had already agreed that anyone who confessed Jesus to be the Messiah would be put out of the synagogue.* (23) *Therefore his parents said, "He is of age; ask him."*

(24) *So for the second time they called the man who had been blind, and they said to him, "Give glory to God! We know that this man is a sinner."* (25) *He answered, "I do not know whether he is a sinner. One thing I do know, that though I was blind, now I see."* (26) *They said to him, "What did he do to you? How did he open your eyes?"* (27) *He answered them, "I have told you already, and you would not listen. Why do you want to hear it again? Do you also want to become his disciples?"* (28) *Then they reviled him, saying, "You are his disciple, but we are disciples of Moses.* (29) *We know that God has spoken to Moses, but as for this man, we do not know where he comes from."* (30) *The man answered, "Here is an astonishing thing! You do not know where he comes from, and yet he opened my eyes.* (31) *We know that God does not listen to sinners, but he does listen to one who worships him and obeys his will.* (32) *Never since the world began has it been heard that anyone opened the eyes of a person born blind.* (33) *If this man were not from God,*

he could do nothing." (34) They answered him, "You were born entirely in sins, and are you trying to teach us?" And they drove him out.

(35) Jesus heard that they had driven him out, and when he found him, he said, "Do you believe in the Son of Man?" (36) He answered, "And who is he, sir? Tell me, so that I may believe in him." (37) Jesus said to him, "You have seen him, and the one speaking with you is he." (38) He said, "Lord, I believe." And he worshiped him. (39) Jesus said, "I came into this world for judgment so that those who do not see may see, and those who do see may become blind." (40) Some of the Pharisees near him heard this and said to him, "Surely we are not blind, are we?" (41) Jesus said to them, "If you were blind, you would not have sin. But now that you say, 'We see,' your sin remains."

Here is another story about a blind man, but this one is in a completely different style from the simple, lyrical narrative of Bartimaeus. This tale is a complex and highly agonistic one. Nevertheless, this one, too, is beautifully crafted, having the intricacy and pace of a dance or a ballet. Its subtle movements are essential to the final outcome, and such is the mastery of the choreographer, or in this case the evangelist, that the underlying structure is not immediately recognizable. In fact its intricacy may only be revealed if we have the opportunity to look again at the whole picture as it plays out in slow motion. But before we begin, we may be alerted to two significant points.

First, in this story, we find the words "blind" or "blind man," and "eyes" or "see," no less than thirty-five times. And, second, this is a reversal story, which means that the normal associations are turned on their head. Normally, blindness indicates an outcast, someone ritually impure, a sinner or a social nobody. Normally, blindness is associated with guilt, while sight—and by extension vision or insight or perception—indicates virtue, or innocence, or righteousness. But in this story Jesus makes a different connection: blindness is associated with innocence or virtue, while sightedness is associated with self-righteousness and sin.

The story begins like so many others, with Jesus "walking along." He is "on the way" again, moving in a determined and deliberate fashion toward the endpoint of his journey. He knows exactly where he is going. The author of John's Gospel always makes a point of noting this clarity of purpose, and in this particular story Jesus' certainty and his authority are almost palpable.

Jesus and his disciples see a blind man, and there follows a mini-theological reflection upon an age-old question: what is the relationship between sickness and sin, or between innocence and suffering? Jesus immediately cuts through the conventional answers and declares that this man's blindness is no indication of previous sin, either his own or that of his forebears. However, the blindness will serve as an opportunity for God's loving concern to become manifest, and it will in due course give way to light, both physically and theologically. The man and some of the crowd, too, will be *enlightened*, their *vision* sharpened, and their *perception* enhanced. But while this theme becomes the more obvious or dominant movement of the ensuing story, there is another movement, set in counterpoint: some people are moving in the opposite direction to the blind man, from sight to blindness, from clarity to darkness, and from perceptiveness to obtuseness. It is a beautifully crafted story and a cautionary tale.

From the outset Jesus takes charge and seizes the initiative. The blind man does not approach and does not even ask to be healed. Jesus, however, will not simply sound a fanfare and perform a miracle. Nor will he deprive people of their dignity. Rather, he will take pains to ensure that this man is involved in his own healing, and he will demonstrate that simple things have a place in God's healing work: spittle, soil, water. At first sight, the image of Jesus spitting on the ground and making some mud with his saliva is perhaps overdrawn, and the man himself does seems a little too complacent. No matter; the gesture serves the dramatic purpose of having Jesus encounter the blind man and begin to redirect his life. "Go," says Jesus, in a typical command. It is, literally, a commissioning or sending forth. The point is underlined by some wordplay: Jesus sends the man to a pool with the curious name "Sent" (v. 7). Perhaps this is the day on which this insignificant pool becomes significant, and named. Or perhaps this is the day its odd name actually makes sense to people who have never understood it up to this moment.

Typically, when Jesus encounters someone, he calls, he heals, and he sends. In this case the sequence is different; in a sense, he sends the man *before* he calls him: "go" precedes "come." In this case the one who is sent is blind, whereas the one who returns is sighted. But then this man is not a sinner like some others who encounter Jesus, and perhaps this is why Jesus is at pains to change his usual pattern. This particular sequence illustrates the passage of an innocent man from blindness to sight, a passage accomplished in two stages: being sent and being recalled. We will soon notice that simultaneously the very opposite sequence is at work, and it is accomplishing the very opposite result. But before we understand that second sequence fully, we are shown how and why it comes about.

We have, then, an unexpected meeting between Jesus and a blind man, followed by a dramatic cure. This encounter is enough to provoke a reaction from a rather motley crowd. First, the man's neighbors and some bystanders establish the identity of the now sighted man, largely on the assertion of the man himself, who explains, to the best of his limited ability, what has happened. He identifies his healer only as "the man called Jesus" (v. 11), and appears not to know Jesus' current whereabouts. Clearly he is not one of Jesus' associates, and in fact he seems a little slow on the uptake. Perhaps the neighbors and bystanders were jealous of the blind man's good fortune. In any event, far from congratulating him, they dragoon him, and bring him before the religious authorities, perhaps seeking to expose him as a fake, or Jesus as a breaker of the Sabbath (v. 16). The man repeats his story to the Pharisees who fall into a dispute about the putative miracle worker: either he is an ungodly charlatan with no respect for the Sabbath or he is indeed a godly person, for how else could blindness have been cured (v. 16)?

From this point on in the story, the sighted man grows in stature, while the Pharisees diminish and grow increasingly frustrated. The man gives public witness (he is, literally, a *martyr*) to Jesus, and from his previously vague reference ("the man called Jesus" [v. 11]), he now identifies Jesus much more explicitly: "He is a prophet," he says (v. 17). The authorities however become even more perverse, refusing to believe either the man, or his parents, or their own common sense. Ironically, given the nature of this story, those who have physical sight are refusing to believe the evidence of their own eyes. They were quick enough to explain his blindness, but are now much slower to account for his restoration.

The man's parents are afraid of several things: of being accused of complicity in fraud, of encouraging the breaking of the Sabbath laws, and of something much worse and harder to identify: of putting their trust and their faith in the unknown healer, which would get them expelled from the synagogue, and perhaps worse. So they try to stay out of the argument by stating that their son knows what had happened, and that his blindness does not mean that he is mentally incompetent. They want him to take all the responsibility: they do not want to get involved. So a second time, the man is questioned, and a second time his questioners appear flustered and incompetent, while the man himself seems to become ever more confident. The Pharisees can only threaten, but the man almost seems to be enjoying the commotion. He intimates that they are less than human because of their willful deafness (v. 27), and even dares to ask, disingenuously, if they want to become disciples. This is the crisis point: the Pharisees actually curse the man and, as he becomes increasingly self-assured and perceptive, they are becoming increasingly enraged and blinded by their own passion.

The Pharisees have clearly overstepped their authority. Cursing, appropriately done, would be the legitimate calling down of God's authority by way of punishment on guilty parties. But in this case the Pharisees have no authority, since the man has done nothing wrong and they have no jurisdiction over him. Technically, they are swearing rather than cursing. What they are doing is *not* legitimate, and puts them clearly in the wrong since the law forbade swearing, slandering, or bad-mouthing others in God's name.

It is clear that these Pharisees are not used to being challenged.

They lay out their rationale, demonstrating that they cannot possibly change their way of thinking, or, ironically, of seeing. In contrast, the now-sighted man lays out his own current understanding, demonstrating that he has been profoundly changed, not only in his way of thinking but especially in his way of seeing things. He challenges the Pharisees' assertion that they do not know where Jesus comes from, playing with language and arguing that it is now self-evident that he comes from God (v. 33). This final assertion, "this man came from God," is the man's third statement about Jesus and, with each additional one he has come a step closer to real faith.

The Pharisees however are not quite finished. Falling back on their theological certainties, they declare that the man was born of sin (*because* he was blind), ask rhetorically if he presumes to think that he can teach them, and then expel him forthwith from the synagogue. These are the actions of frightened men. The threefold irony of course is that their tired theology is just what Jesus came to contest; that indeed the blind man *was* trying to teach them something; and that expulsion from the synagogue is really not the end of the world for someone who had just found Jesus.

Now, almost at the end of the story, Jesus himself re-enters the picture and goes in search of the healed man. He seeks him out, finds him, and puts to him the most important question of his life: "Do you believe in the Son of Man?" (v. 35). It is quite clear that Jesus is looking for faith: this is why he came. Whereupon the man, now on the verge of discipleship, is able to ask urgently, "Tell me, so that I may believe in him" (v. 36). Then Jesus discloses his identity, and the man can now truly look at Jesus and see the Son of Man. "Lord, I believe," he says (v. 38). And he falls on his knees in the time-honored gesture of worshipful faith.

But the story is not over yet. The denouement reveals something about the characters involved in the story, but more important, it points a finger right between the eyes of all of us who encounter it. Jesus states very clearly that blindness and sight are metaphors that can be applied to his whole ministry: "I came to this world for judgment, so that those who do not see may see, and those who do see may become blind" (v. 39). In other words, he came so that those who, *through no fault of their own,* are blind will be restored and healed by God. Then they will have not merely sight but insight and perception. In other words, Jesus also came so that those who, *through sinful arrogance,* make grandiose claims about themselves, will be brought low, if they are not brought to their senses first. Jesus is a sign of contradiction (Lk 2:34).

Illustrating perfectly that none of us can see ourselves as we really are or as God sees us, the Pharisees demonstrate their own arrogance and perversity. "Surely we are not blind, are we?" ("You don't mean that we are blind?" says the Jerusalem Bible), they ask petulantly (v. 40). And the wheel has come full circle: those who claim to be insightful and perceptive are exposed as willfully blind, while the blind but diffident man has been restored to sight, and shown that he has been truly transformed by the experience, since he has now become a believer and an intimate of Jesus.

All who have ever read or heard this story have been invited to identify where they stand with respect to it. We may feel deeply encouraged by the fact that Jesus has encountered us, lifted the scales from our eyes, and restored not just our sight but our self-respect. But in our more graced moments we may also have stopped to ask ourselves: who do I think I am? Do I pose and posture in a self-righteous display of virtue and wisdom like the stereotypical Pharisees? Am I set for a fall unless I acknowledge my own blind spots and humbly return to Jesus and ask that I might see more clearly, and perhaps, even for the very first time?

Maybe it's time for each of us to again practice saying what the blind man said so touchingly—"Lord, I believe"—as if we really meant it.

CHAPTER THIRTEEN

A Memorable Moment

(Mk 14:3-9)[32]

(3) *While he [Jesus] was at Bethany in the house of Simon the leper, as he sat at the table, a woman came with an alabaster jar of very costly ointment of nard, and she broke open the jar and poured the ointment on his head.* (4) *But some were there who said to one another in anger, "Why was the ointment wasted in this way?* (5) *For this ointment could have been sold for more than three hundred denarii, and the money given to the poor."* *And they scolded her.* (6) *But Jesus said, "Let her alone; why do you trouble her? She has performed a good service for me.* (7) *For you always have the poor with you, and you can show kindness to them whenever you wish; but you will not always have me.* (8) *She has done what she could; she has anointed my body beforehand for its burial.* (9) *Truly I tell you, wherever the good news is proclaimed in the whole world, what she has done will be told in remembrance of her."*

There are several stories about a woman, sometimes called Mary, sometimes not named, and sometimes spoken about as being a notorious sinner. These stories have become almost inextricably intertwined, and for many people, Mary Magdalen, Mary the sister of Martha, and the woman who anointed Jesus at Bethany have become merged into a single figure. Many medieval paintings of this scene show a woman with an alabaster jar, and identify her by this single artifact as Mary Magdalen. Some people simply find it all very confusing.

Mark and Matthew both tell the simple story we turn to now. However it is Luke who tells what is essentially the same story, but introduces it by saying the woman "had a bad name in the town" (Lk 7:37). And when John tells it, the main protagonist is Mary the sister of Martha (Jn 12:1–11). Little wonder people have been quick to identify the woman as Mary Magdalen.

In Mark's retelling of the events, there is no indication that the woman was even one of the Marys: she was simply "a woman." Jesus will refer to her four times—perhaps a measure of her significance—without once mentioning her name; and the storyteller gives no indication that we have ever met this woman before. Perhaps we should begin by thinking of her as one of the many nameless people who can stand for *Everywoman* or *Everyman*. There is no need to muddy the waters by calling her Mary and confusing ourselves, but every reason to look deeply into this story for the timeless wisdom it contains.

Jesus is at Bethany (where, of course, his friends Lazarus, Martha, and one of the Marys lived). But on this occasion he was at the house of another friend and acquaintance, Simon the leper. This is a most curious name indeed. Who would want to be identified by a disease or indisposition? Yet who would *not* want to be identified for posterity under circumstances like these. So Simon has his day in the sun, and the context is established. Jesus is the guest, Simon is the host, and Jesus is accepting hospitality rather than giving it. In other words, Jesus is allowing, encouraging Simon, and giving him the "one-up" position that is consistent with a host. Table fellowship (*commensality*) and common meals (*com-pan-ionship*) certainly characterized the ministry of Jesus, but he was not one to seek the limelight, and he knew how to be guest as well as host. It takes a host to show hospitality, but it takes a guest to make a host.

From this point onward in the story, the narrative turns to Jesus, and his words turn to the woman. The disciples are completely marginalized from the story, and Jesus implies that they simply fail to understand either who he is or how his ministry is unfolding. They are in the dark and appear to remain in the dark throughout this entire story. But as the silenced disciples fade from the story, the nameless woman is brought onto center stage. "As he sat at the table, a woman came with an alabaster jar of very costly ointment of nard, and she broke open the jar and poured the ointment on his head" (v. 3). It was certainly dramatic, and it seems to have been quite premeditated: it evidently meant something to her, if to no one else.

There is a certain impetuosity in Jesus' disciples, and they seem very slow to learn to think before they act. True to form, some of them immediately react in a sadly typical, and even timelessly masculine, way (even though they do not otherwise participate in this story, or seem to learn its lessons). Because they do not understand, or maybe because they disagree with some action, they proceed to criticize it— and to scold the woman herself—on completely spurious grounds.

We already met a synagogue official who did not take kindly to Jesus' healing on the Sabbath, telling her to come to be healed on a weekday (Lk 13:14), as if she would have been received any more graciously then. On this occasion, some disciples argue that the ointment could have been sold, and the proceeds given to the poor. It is a specious argument, probably driven by their envy at the woman's intimacy with Jesus, and by the very fact that she had infiltrated the house and literally touched Jesus. It does them no credit at all, and leaves them looking shallow and petulant.

Jesus' attitude is exactly the opposite: encouraging, understanding, indulgent, trusting, attentive. He rebukes the disciples, and comes immediately to her defense: "Let her alone. Why do you trouble her?" (v. 6). It is not only patriarchal societies that, at times, flagrantly abuse authority and foster a climate of criticism and discouragement of those not considered socially significant, though patriarchal societies are particularly prone to going unchecked in such matters. Jesus lived in such a society, but he has strong words for its excesses. On this occasion he criticizes the guests' instinct to belittle and badger, telling them to leave this woman alone and to stop carping and making trouble, fomenting discontent. It is a timely warning and a tender intervention on behalf of the victim.

From this point on, the men of the party, including the host, fade completely from view as the woman becomes the focal point of the story. Jesus concentrates entirely on her, making his fourfold reference to her.

First, "she has performed a good service" ("done a beautiful thing" in the Jerusalem Bible) (v. 6). This is a theologically telling phrase, and not simply a few approving words. Jesus is referring to the "good works" prescribed by the law, and exceeding almsgiving as the most meritorious acts. This woman is commended for an explicitly religious act. Furthermore, the fact that it is directed at Jesus implies that she has personal faith in the one on whose behalf she acts. This nameless woman has, indeed, done "a beautiful thing," and none of Jesus' disciples have as yet even come close to her faith-in-action.

Second, "she has done what she could" (v. 8). This woman has not been persuaded, either by her culture or her friends, that she is utterly powerless or incapable of pleasing God. Whatever her history might have been, she is a woman and therefore virtually insignificant in a social sense. But Jesus commends her for her courage, her integrity, and the strength of her conviction. Too many people react to life's problems as if there is nothing they can do; if each one of them did at least something, as this woman does, the world would be a very different place. But it is much easier to say (and to believe) that there is nothing we can do than it is to look around, seize opportunities, and to act with courage, conscience, and compassion: that, of course, would be to act prophetically.

Third, "she has anointed my body beforehand for its burial" (v. 8). At this point, Jesus raises this woman's faith-filled action to the dignity of a sign or sacrament: something that points far beyond itself and has significance greater than, and beyond, its immediate context. What Jesus says may not be understood by those at the table, but later generations will see her action as anointing Jesus as prophet, priest, and king. It is not only significant for Jesus but also for the person who anoints: this anonymous woman has done a very public and memorable act.

Fourth, then, "what she has done will be told in remembrance of her" ("in memory of her" in the Jerusalem Bible) (v. 9). This powerful phrase is evocative for at least two reasons. In the first place it echoes the other command or invitation of Jesus: that his followers should take bread, break it, and do it in memory of him (see Lk 22:19; 1 Cor 11:25). But it is surely curious that Mark, the author of this story and the earliest of the evangelists, does not actually contain that phrase in the institution text (Mk 14:22–25). Further, it assures future generations of this woman's permanent place in their memory. The repetition of the Eucharist is actually a way of bringing Jesus to mind and physically remembering him; failure to do this in memory of him would be tantamount to forgetting Jesus and, thus, our own Christian identity. All the more impressive then that Jesus should promise that future generations would hold this woman in esteem and keep *her* memory alive. And all the more ironic that, until very recently, the Church appeared to have completely forgotten her, or demeaned or marginalized her yet again (the "Mary Magdalene syndrome"). If we take Jesus seriously, this woman has an irreplaceable part to play—personally and symbolically—in the life of the Christian community. Her memory has recently been revived, particularly by feminist theologians,[33] but her significance is once more in danger of being eclipsed. This story must be told and retold in our time; her memory must not be allowed to lapse.

Jesus said that the last would be first, and this encounter illustrates the significance of such a promise: this nonentity, this "nobody" becomes a model of living faith, and as such is rewarded by Jesus, just as he promised.

Two other points are worth noting. Taking up the disciples' observation—that the ointment could have been sold and the money given to the poor—Jesus says: "For you always have the poor with you, and you can show kindness to them whenever you wish; but you will not always have me" (v. 7). It is as if Jesus is acknowledging the validity of the disciples' point as far as it goes, yet he is going beyond their own limited reasoning. The poor are a social constant, and almsgiving as a religious responsibility will never cease to apply, but over and above this usual and continual duty, one should be sensitive to recognizing the claim of the exceptional. This is an exceptional case: Jesus is deserving, and thus worthy, of the woman's piety, while her action appropriately draws attention to this moment when the Son of Man is symbolically (and proleptically, or ahead of time), anointed for his burial. This is a theological teaching moment and it is exceptionally significant.

The other point is this: Jesus says that "wherever the good news is proclaimed in the whole world" (v. 9), this occasion and the woman at its center will be remembered. Again, this promise is pointing forward to a time when the disciples of Jesus would fulfill the mandate that they had not yet received and certainly were, as yet, unable to comprehend. Mark's community would have been kept in mind, through the retelling of this story, of the implications of faith in Jesus: it should lead to a ministry beyond local communities, and a ministry by disciples of Jesus that would explicitly include women.

The statement of Jesus also presages a similar but centrally important statement at the end of Matthew's Gospel where, after the Resurrection, Jesus tells the Eleven to go into the whole world, and promises to be with them when they do so (Mt 28:19–20). That statement is already incorporated into the coda added to Mark's own Gospel in which Jesus says, "Go into all the world and proclaim the good news to the whole creation" (16:15); Luke's Gospel also concludes on a similar note of universal mission (Lk 24:47). These reflections must inevitably lead us to inquire further about the historicity of Mark's account of the memorable woman and, in consequence, to continue the critical discussion about women and ministry in the contemporary Church of today.

This was indeed a memorable evening for the woman and for posterity, if not immediately for the disciples. For we who strive to learn from Jesus' encounters and to be faithful to his commissioning, it does us no harm to remember how he is portrayed in this story: approachable, relaxed, responsive to loving gestures, encouraging of signs of faith, gracious and welcoming, and supportive of invisible people and victims.

The woman, it should be noted, is present, is attentive, and ministers. But throughout the dramatic and undoubtedly faith-filled encounter, she never says a single word.

Endnotes

32. Also see Matthew 26:6–13. Compare Luke 7:36–50 and John 12:1–8.
33. Notably, Elizabeth Schussler-Fiorenza, *In Memory of Her: A Feminist Theological Reconstruction of Christian Origins*. New York: Crossroad, 1983.

CHAPTER FOURTEEN

A Man Up a Tree

(Lk 19:1–10)

(1) *He [Jesus] entered Jericho and was passing through it.* (2) *A man was there named Zacchaeus; he was a chief tax collector and was rich.* (3) *He was trying to see who Jesus was, but on account of the crowd he could not, because he was short in stature.* (4) *So he ran ahead and climbed a sycamore tree to see him, because he was going to pass that way.* (5) *When Jesus came to the place, he looked up and said to him, "Zacchaeus, hurry and come down; for I must stay at your house today."* (6) *So he hurried down and was happy to welcome him.* (7) *All who saw it began to grumble and said, "He has gone to be the guest of one who is a sinner."* (8) *Zacchaeus stood there and said to the Lord, "Look, half of my possessions, Lord, I will give to the poor; and if I have defrauded anyone of anything, I will pay back four times as much."* (9) *Then Jesus said to him, "Today salvation has come to this house, because he too is a son of Abraham.* (10) *For the Son of Man came to seek out and to save the lost."*

Zacchaeus was a little man, diminutive even. Like many short men, he was ambitious: he wanted to amount to something, to go up in the world, to be a man of stature, a big man. And he had certainly succeeded in making something of his life, for he was "a chief tax collector and was rich" (v. 2). But all this had cost him his reputation, for he was in the employ of the occupying Roman forces and therefore not a man with a wide circle of friends, unlike the centurion (Lk 7:1–10), who was exceptional. The little rich man would have been despised both by the Jews, who were forced to pay taxes, and even by his fellow tax collectors, for he lived in a dog-eat-dog world.

Still there was something about Zacchaeus, some latent potential, that made him far from insignificant or worthless. He was capable of making a difference, for good as much as for ill, because he had initiative, curiosity, and a good heart. He was by no means a hopeless case. In fact, he was goodness just waiting to happen.

Every authentic human encounter requires that both parties be displaced, that the trajectories of their lives change in such a way that those trajectories converge. Prior to an encounter, lives are lived separately, independently. After any authentic encounter they are mutually related, interwoven. Zacchaeus was about to have a true encounter with Jesus and with destiny.

One day Jesus was passing through town; but, at this stage of his life, he was not able to pass unnoticed. He had cured Bartimaeus not long before[34] and, now, a motley crowd was rapidly gathering—the curious, the sympathetic, and those who just happened to be there. They must have created enough disturbance so that Zacchaeus, despite being preoccupied with his own concerns, could not fail to notice the commotion. Was he curious or sympathetic, or did he, too, just happen to be there? He may have been there by chance but he was certainly curious, and his curiosity got the better of him and changed his life.

Here is a man with a creative mind and the spirit of a risk-taker. Zacchaeus is not content just to question the crowd for information (they may not have been too forthcoming anyway), and evidently disinclined to push and shove. But due to his short stature he is likely to miss catching sight of the passing celebrity, Jesus. However, the events of the next few minutes will demonstrate that Zacchaeus was moved as much by grace as by curiosity, and that he wanted more than simply to see; like Bartimaeus, he was striving for insight, for perception, for a level of experience that few people dream of and even fewer attain. The story tells us that he was "trying to see who Jesus was" (but once again, the Jerusalem Bible version states it slightly differently, saying that "he was anxious to see what kind of man Jesus was") (v. 3). It was his anxiousness that raised him above the level of a curious bystander and ensured that he found the perfect vantage point.

Resourceful Zacchaeus then, spying a likely sycamore tree and wrapping his dignity and his loose robe around him, ran ahead of the crowd and scrambled up the tree. Sycamore trees are very easy to climb, as small boys know. But first you have to catch a hold of the lowest branch and pull yourself up to where it joins the trunk, and that is not always a simple matter: the lowest branch is often too high for a small boy. Sometimes you just have to jump. Zacchaeus was lucky. But he could so easily have failed miserably and finished up flat on his back or in an undignified heap. There is something rather attractive about a risk-taker.

Up in the tree, and just in time, for Jesus is getting close, Zacchaeus must have been very pleased with himself. He could observe without being seen, and he could see without needing to respond by committing himself; the story tells us that he wanted to *see* Jesus, not that he wanted to be seen by Jesus, and certainly not that he wanted a personal, public encounter. So there he is, perfectly placed, yet unnoticed by anyone.

But suddenly everything is changed, and his plans, such as they were, now count for nothing. Jesus was indeed passing by, and Zacchaeus did indeed have a sycamore-tree-perfect view. But quite unexpectedly, Jesus stopped, looked up, saw Zacchaeus and made a point of addressing him. How utterly embarrassing for the little man. There he was, in full view of everyone, and quite incapable of escaping, either swiftly or gracefully. Suddenly, from being in control and watching life from a safe distance, Zacchaeus must have felt that things were now completely out of his control. Not only did Jesus notice him; not only did Jesus address him; Jesus actually invited himself to be Zacchaeus's guest!

Details such as these have become unforgettable memories for generations of Christians and others: Jesus noticed, Jesus cared, and Jesus called. If it could happen to Zacchaeus, could it not happen to

anyone, even one of us? It is encouraging to acknowledge that many
of Jesus' disciples—today as much as when he walked the road to Jericho—have responded to the initiative of Jesus rather than trying to
wrest the initiative themselves.

In the agonistic Mediterranean culture of the time, everyone
would immediately know that by calling to Zacchaeus in this way,
Jesus was issuing a kind of challenge that could not be taken lightly. If
Zacchaeus did not respond appropriately he would be publicly humiliated. But there was a strange twist to this particular challenge.
Jesus rarely played by the conventional cultural rules and was unim-
pressed by the almost obsessive cultural need to make social capital at
every turn. So why did he both challenge Zacchaeus to demonstrate
his openhanded hospitality and risk losing face himself? The people
clearly knew Zacchaeus to be a quisling, an enemy of the people, a
lackey of a foreign power. So what is Jesus driving at when he deliberately invites himself to stay with this man whom the people identified
as a sinner (v. 7)?

We know that Jesus seemed almost to take delight in thumbing
his nose at convention: far from losing face by associating with someone like Zacchaeus, Jesus was about to raise the tax-collector's status
by a kind of "reverse flow": his own popularity and acquired social
status would ensure that Zacchaeus's standing among the people would
be enhanced. Jesus is using his own social capital deliberately to affirm the little man.

But the people are not only perfectly aware of Jesus' favoritism
for the tax collector; they are incensed by his choice of "a sinner" as
his host for the night. No sooner had Zacchaeus jumped down from
the tree and offered Jesus a verbal welcome than he feels the insults of
the people which, in fact, seem to indicate their disappointment in
Jesus, as much as their animosity toward the tax collector. This is not
the first time there was grumbling; previously, the scribes and Pharisees had done the same, because "all the tax collectors and sinners
were coming near to listen to him" ("seeking his company" says the
Jerusalem Bible) (Lk 15:1).

Interestingly, Zacchaeus is not intimidated by the people. Nor does he try to ignore them. The story goes on to say that he "stood his ground" (v. 8 in the Jerusalem Bible version), turning to Jesus with a statement that compromised him in the face of the crowd, and evidently won Jesus' unmitigated approval. The little man's quick thinking and resolve are astounding. Hardly has he landed on his feet before he is making the kind of promises that could make people conclude that he is completely out of his mind. But of course he is not: Zacchaeus has undergone a profound conversion, and he is certainly not crazy.

He declares, generously, even profligately, that he will give half of his possessions to the poor. This is quite astounding by any standards, but particularly for a man whose professional existence has placed him in direct opposition to the poor. Zacchaeus certainly could not have been a successful tax collector if he had been indulgent to the poor. His very success indicates that he must have exploited and alienated them. And now he is saying—in public and for all to hear—that he will give half of his possessions to the poor. Half! To the poor! It is too much, too expansive a gesture. It might have been understandable if he gave a donation to the Temple, but to *the poor*! It begins to look as though Zacchaeus might well have kept the Jewish laws even though he was not a pious Jew, for Tobit 4:10–11 assures people that "almsgiving delivers from death…almsgiving is an excellent offering in the presence of the Most High."

But Zacchaeus is not finished. He continues to compromise himself and his security by undertaking to compensate *anyone* he has defrauded, not just according to the letter of the law—which required twofold compensation—but by a factor of four: he will repay every injustice fourfold. This arrangement echoes Exodus 22:1 and was not unknown in Roman law, and if Zacchaeus was aware of it then he is a far more serious person than we might at first assume.

Here is a man who is making radical changes to his life. Generous philanthropists and humanitarians would never contemplate giving away half their substance. Even if we could imagine one who actually did that, such bounteousness pales by comparison with the gesture of Zacchaeus, who promises *in addition* this astounding fourfold compensation. This is going to compromise his whole life: those people will be lining up at his house, looking for money. It is quite staggering to imagine the significance of his action. Rich people simply do not behave this way. But then Jesus would remind the people—mostly the poor people—just how difficult it would be for rich people to gain entrance into the Kingdom, or Realm of God. Zacchaeus is actually one of the very few (apparent) exceptions we encounter in the New Testament. It is an *apparent* exception because, by the time Zacchaeus is finished he will be significantly less rich than before. His principal will have shrunk considerably. Which simply proves the rule.

From anxious curiosity to bold tree-climbing, and from a profound encounter to radical conversion, Zacchaeus has had an exciting day. But it is not over yet. As he stands between a gracious Jesus and a complaining crowd, he hears words that raise his status infinitely more than he could ever have imagined, and truly make a man of him: he is called a "son of Abraham" (v. 9). For all the public scandal of his life and profession, for all his being regarded as an outcast by pious Jews, and for all his riches, Zacchaeus is more than the sum of his sins. He understands almsgiving and restitution, he is willing to admit his errant ways, and he is committed to his own conversion. Zacchaeus is truly a son of Abraham on this blessed day because he has begun to act justly, love kindness, and walk humbly with God (see Mic 6:8).

In the same breath as he calls Zacchaeus a son of Abraham, Jesus asserts that Zacchaeus has encountered salvation—and not some future salvation but salvation right now, right where he is. This is Jesus at his most magisterial and yet most simple; he declares that this is exactly why he came, and today is a profoundly significant day for him, too. He has come precisely "to seek out and save the lost" (v. 9).

And so we realize, finally, that notwithstanding all Zacchaeus's initiative and risk-taking, it was actually Jesus who sought him out, caught his eye as he sat in the tree, and *called him by name.* This is a measure of God's intimacy. It is the way lost souls are saved. It is amazing grace indeed.

After all that, Zacchaeus—like some other people we have observed in these encounters—never did explicitly confess faith in Jesus. But he certainly *expressed* it in action.

Endnotes

34. In Luke's account that we follow here, the Zacchaeus story follows hard on the heels of a story of an unnamed blind beggar near Jericho. Compare it to the Bartimaeus story in Mark 10.

CHAPTER FIFTEEN

A Well-Woman

(Jn 4:1-42)[35]

(1) *Now when Jesus learned that the Pharisees had heard, "Jesus is making and baptizing more disciples than John"—* (2) *although it was not Jesus himself but his disciples who baptized—*(3) *he left Judea and started back to Galilee.* (4) *But he had to go through Samaria.* (5) *So he came to a Samaritan city called Sychar, near the plot of ground that Jacob had given to his son Joseph.* (6) *Jacob's well was there, and Jesus, tired out by his journey, was sitting by the well. It was about noon.*

(7) *A Samaritan woman came to draw water, and Jesus said to her, "Give me a drink."* (8) *(His disciples had gone to the city to buy food.)* (9) *The Samaritan woman said to him, "How is it that you, a Jew, ask a drink of me, a woman of Samaria?" (Jews do not share things in common with Samaritans.)* (10) *Jesus answered her, "If you knew the gift of God, and who it is that is saying to you, 'Give me a drink,' you would have asked him, and he would have given you living water."* (11) *The woman said to him, "Sir, you have no bucket, and the well is deep. Where do you get that living water?* (12) *Are you greater than our ancestor Jacob, who gave us the well, and with his sons and his flocks drank from it?"* (13) *Jesus said to her, "Everyone who drinks of this water will be thirsty again,* (14) *but those who drink of the water that I will give them will never be thirsty. The water that I will give will become in them a spring of water gushing up to eternal life."* (15) *The woman said to him, "Sir, give me*

this water, so that I may never be thirsty or have to keep coming here to draw water."

(16) *Jesus said to her, "Go, call your husband, and come back." (17) The woman answered him, "I have no husband." Jesus said to her, "You are right in saying, 'I have no husband'; (18) for you have had five husbands, and the one you have now is not your husband. What you have said is true!" (19) The woman said to him, "Sir, I see that you are a prophet. (20) Our ancestors worshiped on this mountain, but you say that the place where people must worship is in Jerusalem." (21) Jesus said to her, "Woman, believe me, the hour is coming when you will worship the Father neither on this mountain nor in Jerusalem. (22) You worship what you do not know; we worship what we know, for salvation is from the Jews. (23) But the hour is coming, and is now here, when the true worshipers will worship the Father in spirit and truth, for the Father seeks such as these to worship him. (24) God is spirit, and those who worship him must worship in spirit and truth." (25) The woman said to him, "I know that Messiah is coming" (who is called Christ). "When he comes, he will proclaim all things to us." (26) Jesus said to her, "I am he, the one who is speaking to you."*

(27) *Just then his disciples came. They were astonished that he was speaking with a woman, but no one said, "What do you want?" or, "Why are you speaking with her?" (28) Then the woman left her water jar and went back to the city. She said to the people, (29) "Come and see a man who told me everything I have ever done! He cannot be the Messiah, can he?" (30) They left the city and were on their way to him.*

(31) *Meanwhile the disciples were urging him, "Rabbi, eat something." (32) But he said to them, "I have food to eat that you do not know about." (33) So the disciples said to one another, "Surely no one has brought him something to eat?" (34) Jesus said to them, "My food is to do the will of him who sent me and to complete his work. (35) Do you not say, 'Four months more, then comes the harvest'? But I tell you, look around you, and*

see how the fields are ripe for harvesting. (36) *The reaper is already receiving wages and is gathering fruit for eternal life, so that sower and reaper may rejoice together.* (37) *For here the saying holds true, 'One sows and another reaps.'* (38) *I sent you to reap that for which you did not labor. Others have labored, and you have entered into their labor."*

(39) *Many Samaritans from that city believed in him because of the woman's testimony, "He told me everything I have ever done."* (40) *So when the Samaritans came to him, they asked him to stay with them; and he stayed there two days.* (41) *And many more believed because of his word.* (42) *They said to the woman, "It is no longer because of what you said that we believe, for we have heard for ourselves, and we know that this is truly the Savior of the world."*

Here is an encounter in three movements. It develops like a symphony and, like an Unfinished Symphony, it leaves us to ponder on what might have happened next. But if we pay careful attention to its three Movements, we may be able to apply some lessons from the unnamed woman's experience, and also learn something about how one apparently insignificant person can have a profound effect upon many more.

Jesus is tired. He is on the way back "home" to Galilee from Judea. The story tells us that he "had to go through Samaria" (v. 4), but the need, or imperative, was moral rather than physical: he could well have bypassed Samaria, but evidently chose not to. For whatever reason then, Jesus was once again crossing boundaries, going into unfamiliar or alien territory, situating himself as a stranger in relation to those he would meet. This is an intrinsically tiring enterprise, and by the time Jesus reached Jacob's well he would have been more than ready to sit down and rest (v. 6). How many times we have noticed his tiredness and been reminded of the excessive demands made upon him when he is tired.

The most dominant tone in the First Movement is the phrase "if (the Jerusalem Bible adds 'only') you knew" (v. 10). Jesus will disclose himself to an unsuspecting woman, and is almost wishing her to discover his significance for her life. He is determined to encounter this particular Samaritan, for as soon as she appears he says, rather abruptly, "Give me a drink." He was, after all, a stranger passing through; he had no bucket and therefore the water was inaccessible; and he was thirsty. He must rely on this woman for a drink, but he is unlikely to get one unless he initiates a conversation. Given who she is, she is not at all likely to engage him in conversation. But by acknowledging his position of social inferiority as an outsider or stranger, he subtly enhances her position as an insider, or host, even though there is a clear difference in their respective social status. The woman immediately identifies this difference, contrasting "you, a Jew[ish man]," and "me, a woman of Samaria" (v. 9).

Her question ("Why ask me for a drink?") will be answered immediately and cryptically: "If you knew the gift of God," says Jesus (or in the Jerusalem Bible, a more urgent "If you only knew what God is offering") (v. 10). Of course Jesus intends to let her know exactly what God is offering. Jesus offers water of his own; but though he is addressing the woman, his offer is for all, for anyone and everyone ("everyone who drinks" [v. 13]; "those who drink" [v. 14]); he has already begun to *evangelize*, to proclaim good news for anyone and everyone. His message is inclusive and universal, and it is a promise of "a spring of water gushing up to eternal life" (v. 14). There are two significant points. First, he offers water that springs up, or gushes up. This verb is not used anywhere else in the gospels, and it refers primarily to a person who is overjoyed, literally "springing" or "jumping" for joy. The water will be like this. So a person will not even need a bucket because the water will gush up and be immediately accessible. And second, the offer is for nothing other than "eternal life."

"If [only] you knew the gift of God," says Jesus. He will later show her that he himself is the gift (vv. 16–30). Indeed he is not talking about an object, some gift that God gives, but about the very self-gift[ing] of God. God is the gift; the gift is God. This is the first thing the woman needs, and the second is simply an extension or illustration of the first: she needs the one who is speaking with her.

Some people imagine eternal life as a future reality, too shadowy to have much real meaning. Jesus is speaking of something quite different, something that is already beginning now. (We also saw that in his encounter with Zacchaeus.) But Jesus is not offering eternal bliss after death: his offer—to "all," "whoever," or "those who" drink of the water he offers—is of something that is operative immediately and that "will become in them a spring" (v. 14).

The First Movement ends with the woman intrigued. But she and Jesus are actually at cross-purposes; and though she is by no means hostile, she is somewhat guarded—or perhaps frivolous—and does not yet have faith. Not by any means.

In the course of the Second Movement, Jesus explains more about the gift he is offering and reveals his identity. But there are other themes and harmonies, and they relate to the woman herself. Jesus shows, first, that he knows her intimately (v. 18). He commends her truthfulness, twice, and shows that he understands her irregular situation. But his intention is neither to condemn her, nor to dwell on the past. He shows no inclination to condemn, only to enlighten, to encourage, and to commission. So typical of Jesus is this positive approach that we should take it seriously as we apply it to ourselves.

The combination of Jesus' knowledge of the woman and her own admission of her circumstances (v. 17) mark the beginning of her conversion: her turning away from her own past and turning to Jesus. Without any further delay, Jesus invites her directly: "Woman, believe me," he says (v. 21). He addresses her with a term of respect, and without a shadow of condescension, and he calls her to an authentic, personal encounter with him. He asks her to believe *him*, not simply to believe his words: this is much more demanding. It must have been startling for her; she had most likely had plenty of relationships, but no true encounters up to this point in her life. By the time Jesus finished his instruction (vv. 21–24), the woman was still attentive, and when she declared her belief in the coming Messiah, Jesus disclosed his true identity.

"I am he," or "I am the one," or "I AM WHO AM," seem rather odd ways for him to identify himself. It could be (I base this on an experience in West Africa and the language of the people there) that Jesus is saying effectively, "It's me," just as Yahweh said to Moses or Jesus revealed to his disciples. Anyone who says, "It's me" (in response to the question "who's there?" or "who are you?"), clearly knows that the questioner will recognize his or her voice. No one says, "It's me," unless they are expecting to be recognized. This means, of course, some previous encounter, or an enduring memory, on the part of the questioner.

In the present instance, the implication—or the tantalizing suggestion—is that the woman recognizes Jesus from the past. "I AM" ("It's me") is revealing himself as "the Messiah, the Christ," whom she has already experienced, dimly through the faith she professes. The Second Movement ends with Jesus' declaration: "I AM...speaking with you" (v. 26), and the woman is brought to faith in the person before her.

The Third Movement opens in a minor key: the disciples, who have missed the whole thing, are dumbfounded when they see Jesus with the woman (v. 27). True to form, no one mentions it, but clearly they had missed one of the most significant episodes of Jesus' life. And *they* were his disciples.

The woman disappears, leaving her water jar behind. Either this is rank forgetfulness or her agenda has been so changed that was what originally important is quite insignificant now. But it stands as a challenge to us: do we cling to our own agenda, or are we willing to change when circumstances warrant? What is the water jug we carry to and fro? Is it possible that we might be persuaded to leave it behind because there are more important things in life? What might such important things be? How will we know? There is another possibility, though: did she unconsciously know she had "forgotten" her water jar because she wanted to return to the well to encounter Jesus again?

Returning to the town without her water jug must have made the woman rather conspicuous—and vulnerable. But she had a message to convey, and she seems totally unselfconscious now. She calls the townsfolk to "come and see" the stranger, and she even suggests, rhetorically, that he might be the Messiah. It is enough to pique the curiosity of the community, which seems to have set off, immediately, and en masse. But there is some hesitation: the verb (in the imperfect tense) tells us that "they left the city and *were on their way* [italics added] to him" rather than that they left in a hurry to encounter Jesus. Thus, they seem to be tentative and not yet committed. Nevertheless, they were indeed "on the way" to Jesus. It is an encouraging sign for them, but also a sign that the woman has now become credible to her own people. Any previous indications suggested that she had absolutely no credibility, so her encounter with Jesus must have been quite transformative.

By now, the woman herself is coming to faith. She began by referring to Jesus as "you." Then, she called him by the more respectful title, "sir" (v. 11). The next time she addresses him, she has softened her tone and not only calls him "sir," but indicates her willingness to be in some degree of indebtedness to him: "Sir, give me this water so that I may never be thirsty" (v. 15). By the time the disciples of Jesus return, she has indicated to the townspeople her growing conviction about who Jesus might actually be, and she uses the word "Messiah" (v. 29). Now the disciples return, and they address Jesus only as "Rabbi," teacher (v. 31). They are far behind the woman in their progress to faith. They have not encountered him as profoundly as she has, and it will soon be clear that she has, indeed, come to faith and brought her neighbors to faith as well (v. 42).

Meanwhile, Jesus must patiently explain to the disciples that he does not need their food: he has "food to eat that you do not know about" (v. 32). The evangelist portrays them as exceedingly slow witted, but they are a foil to Jesus, who proceeds to explain—for the first time in John's Gospel—the nature of his missionary ministry: his "food" is to do the will of the one who sent him, and complete God's work (v. 34). What, we might ask, is that work? Given the situation in which Jesus finds himself, his work would seem to be precisely this: to find himself in Samaria, doing non-Jewish things with non-Jewish people, because "he had to" (v. 4). So what is our own way of doing God's will? What and where is our own Samaria? Who are the people we should be with, and what unexpected or unconventional things might we be called upon to do? Sometimes our imagination fails and we flounder, or try to change our location, rather than seeking and finding the God who calls, wherever we may be.

Jesus tells the people that the harvest is now. "Look around you," he says (v. 35). People often think the harvest is a long way off, but Jesus is telling people that now is the important time: "The hour is coming, and is now here" (v. 23). Others have sown—John the Baptist and Jesus particularly—and the disciples are sent to reap, to gather the harvest (v. 38) they did not work for. The fruits of mission are already ripe: God has been working among the Samaritans, Jesus has continued the work, and the Samaritan woman herself has had a part to play. Now the disciples, who were absent most of the time the drama was unfolding, are invited to reap. The question for us, perhaps, is this: can we see how others have labored before us, and how indebted we are to them? Can we perceive the harvest and remain working in the fields faithfully to the end?

But the Samaritan woman and her townspeople have the last word: the people believed because of her public witness (she proclaimed to them; she too was a martyr, one who bore witness to the faith she professed); and most of the community ("many more"—v. 41) came to believe Jesus through actually hearing the Word themselves, through her mediation.

We may make two concluding observations. First, the Gerasenes had begged Jesus to leave after he liberated one of their community (Mk 5:17). Here the Samaritans offer a striking contrast: they beg him to stay with them, and he does so. Their openness, curiosity, and incipient godliness bore fruit in abundance. If only the Gerasenes had known who was speaking with them. This was Jesus' hope for the Samaritans (v. 10), and it was realized. If only *we* knew. If only *we* lived as if we knew.

And, second, the people finally believe, not only on the basis of the woman, but because of Jesus himself. However, the woman in this case had been instrumental: "many Samaritans believed because of the woman's testimony" (v. 39). Evidently, the people of this Samaritan village were more open to a woman's testimony—even a scandalous woman's testimony—than would prove to be the case later among the good disciples of Jesus: they would refuse to believe their women's testimony about the Resurrection, judging it to be "an idle tale" ("pure nonsense" in the Jerusalem Bible) (Lk 24:11).

Endnotes

35. Like the story of the man born blind, this account only occurs in John's Gospel. I gave it this title, "A Well-Woman," because of the associations with the well and with wellness and because it provides an interesting contrast with the "Bent-Over Woman" in Luke 13:10–17.

CHAPTER SIXTEEN

The Gift of a Stranger

(Lk 24:13–35)

(13) *Now on that same day [of the Resurrection] two of them were going to a village called Emmaus, about seven miles from Jerusalem,* (14) *and talking with each other about all these things that had happened.* (15) *While they were talking and discussing, Jesus himself came near and went with them,* (16) *but their eyes were kept from recognizing him.* (17) *And he said to them, "What are you discussing with each other while you walk along?" They stood still, looking sad.* (18) *Then one of them, whose name was Cleopas, answered him, "Are you the only stranger in Jerusalem who does not know the things that have taken place there in these days?"* (19) *He asked them, "What things?" They replied, "The things about Jesus of Nazareth, who was a prophet mighty in deed and word before God and all the people,* (20) *and how our chief priests and leaders handed him over to be condemned to death and crucified him.* (21) *But we had hoped that he was the one to redeem Israel. Yes, and besides all this, it is now the third day since these things took place.* (22) *Moreover, some women of our group astounded us. They were at the tomb early this morning,* (23) *and when they did not find his body there, they came back and told us that they had indeed seen a vision of angels who said that he was alive.* (24) *Some of those who were with us went to the tomb and found it just as the women had said; but they did not see him."* (25) *Then he said to them, "Oh, how foolish you are, and how slow of heart to believe all*

that the prophets have declared! (26) *Was it not necessary that the Messiah should suffer these things and then enter into his glory?"* (27) *Then beginning with Moses and all the prophets, he interpreted to them the things about himself in all the scriptures.*

(28) *As they came near the village to which they were going, he walked ahead as if he were going on.* (29) *But they urged him strongly, saying, "Stay with us, because it is almost evening and the day is now nearly over." So he went in to stay with them.* (30) *When he was at the table with them, he took bread, blessed and broke it, and gave it to them.* (31) *Then their eyes were opened, and they recognized him; and he vanished from their sight.* (32) *They said to each other, "Were not our hearts burning within us while he was talking to us on the road, while he was opening the scriptures to us?"* (33) *That same hour they got up and returned to Jerusalem; and they found the eleven and their companions gathered together.* (34) *They were saying, "The Lord has risen indeed, and he has appeared to Simon!"* (35) *Then they told what had happened on the road, and how he had been made known to them in the breaking of the bread.*

Luke is sometimes called the evangelist of mission. He, above all, shows how people's worlds are turned inside out: from being self-focused or inverted, people discover that life is to be lived for others, that they are called to self-transcendence, and that the meaning of discipleship is mission. Bartimaeus had spent years watching life pass him by, living on the margin, sitting by the side of the road. Zacchaeus had attempted to gather rather than to share and had succeeded in accumulating money but losing friends. The Samaritan woman had settled for shame and survival, and the Gerasene demoniac for a twilight life of graveyards and slow self-destruction. All of these, and many, many more, were encountered by Jesus, and many had their lives turned around, and were sent on mission—or co-missioned—as disciples and proclaimers of the realm of God.

Mission is godly work because mission is the work of God. But by God's Providence, what was brought down to earth in Jesus has been continued on earth since Jesus' time by those commissioned by baptism and convinced that such commissioning represents God's urgent invitation to collaboration for the sake of all humanity. The story we are about to ponder shows how dispirited people can be filled with God's Spirit, how people who search for meaning may find it, and how those who have discovered life's *why* can bear any *how* (as Friedrich Nietzsche said) in life.

Two of the disciples, whose conversion story we do not know, may have been steadfast for a while, but had evidently been brought to the brink of despair and had turned away from Jerusalem and the hope it once represented. Not that they did not have some reason to give up: Jesus had been captured, summarily tried, condemned, crucified, killed, and hurriedly but certainly buried. Now, on the third day after this humiliating anticlimax, and despite rumors that they simply could not countenance, they were leaving town for good. It was the first day of the week, the Sabbath; but for them there was no rest, no rejoicing, no worship, and certainly no jubilee on this Sabbath day.

These two disciples then are in deep conversation as they leave Jerusalem and head for Emmaus, a seven-mile walk that would take them a couple of hours. Their evident trauma illustrates just how strong their commitment had been and just how broken were their hopes. They seem to have lost their reason for living. At some point, they notice a stranger walking alongside them. Either they are walking very slowly, because of the intensity of their conversation, or the stranger is in something of a hurry. However the three actually converge, it is the stranger who opens the conversation with a curious question: "What are you discussing?" (v. 17). It must have been his tone that softened this otherwise rather impertinent question, for surely it was asked with concern and compassion. Even so, it is odd for a stranger to initiate a conversation in this way, and odder still that he should so directly insert himself into their private dialogue. Luke's text does not tell us exactly how they responded, but it does indicate their mood: "They stood still, looking sad" (v. 17).

These people seem so utterly dispirited that they have, literally, nothing to say for themselves. The Jerusalem Bible tells us, "They stopped short, their faces downcast." In today's language, we would say they were depressed, and understandably so. Yet they were not out of touch with reality, for when Cleopas finally responds, he indicates that the death of Jesus was common knowledge. Not, apparently to Jesus; or is he just carrying on a charade? Jesus innocently asks for further clarification, and the pair—in unison like a Greek chorus—share their faith.

Cleopas is named, while his companion remains nameless. Perhaps this is a conventional way of indicating a married couple. If so, what should we make of the fact that they acknowledge that "some women from our group astounded us" (v. 22) by encountering an empty tomb and claiming to have seen angels who declared Jesus to be alive? They are quite clear that they have heard astoundingly good news about Jesus, yet allow themselves to discount it, apparently because it was only women's testimony. Even worse, they have actually had this "unreliable" testimony corroborated by some friends—presumably men, and therefore presumably reliable—yet they still fail to take it seriously. What kind of faith can they possibly have?

They appear to believe quite firmly that Jesus "was a prophet mighty in deed and word (or, as the Jerusalem Bible says, "proved that he was a great prophet") before God and all the people" (v. 19). Furthermore, they had hoped "that he was the one to redeem Israel" (v. 21). So are they simply fair-weather friends, lacking the courage of their own convictions or have the past few days' events so traumatized them that they are still quite dazed and incapable of thinking with any consistency? It appears to be the latter, and one can perhaps therefore sympathize with Cleopas and his companion.

Why, then, is Jesus' immediate response so harsh-sounding? He says, "Oh, how foolish [*anoētoi* meaning "mindless, out of mind"] you are!" (v. 25). Perhaps, Jesus is berating them specifically for their lack of faith. We know that he is always looking for faith, particularly among the people of Israel and, most particularly, among his own disciples. Yet often he fails to find it. On this occasion, he criticizes them for being so "slow of heart to believe" (v. 25) despite the fact that the prophets had clearly indicated that God's Anointed One ("the Christ") would "suffer and then enter into his glory" (v. 26). But his criticism was also tempered with patient teaching, and his talk of mindlessness was apparently not taken literally. Jesus proceeded to give them a refresher course in sacred Scripture in order to help them see what they had overlooked.

The disciples were evidently impressed and edified, for when the little group of three reached their intended destination they were already fast friends. Jesus, who had earlier appeared out of nowhere, now seemed content to disappear into the distance. He began to separate from them, as if intending to continue his journey. Cleopas and his companion had to press Jesus into being their guest. Having been very much the initiator and giver in this developing relationship, the stranger now seemed quite willing to become more of a guest. But further surprises were in store for the disciples.

First, Jesus the guest began to increasingly act like a host. As they sat down at the table, it was Jesus who took the bread in his hands and proceeded to say the blessing. Then, just as deliberately and with deep meaning, it was Jesus who broke it and handed it to each of them. Not only was this the prerogative of a host, it was an action that had characterized the feeding of the five thousand and the four thousand (see Mk 6:30–44; 8:1–10. Mt 14:13–21; 15:32–39. Lk 9:10–17. Jn 6:1–13). It also would have been familiar to the disciples from their religious gatherings, but perhaps at this moment they were particularly reminded of those famous feedings.

Evidently by the time this story came to be edited by Luke, the early Christian community would also have reflected upon the action of the Last Supper, and its reiteration in the first eucharistic celebrations. Nevertheless, the heart of Luke's Emmaus account is this simple and profound fourfold action of taking, blessing, breaking, and sharing. And this seems to be the trigger that releases the disciples from their stupor.

With a wonderfully dramatic touch, Luke tells us that in that very moment—when bread given became bread received, when the diners became companions, sharers of bread—they recognized Jesus for the first time. *But "he [had already] vanished from their sight"* (v. 31). By the time they came to their senses and realized what was happening, the elusive stranger-guest-companion was no longer there, though the effect of his presence was certainly apparent. He was there in the broken bread in their trembling hands. He was there in their keen mind's eye. He was there in their ringing ears and in their burning hearts. Excitedly they shared with each other the experience of those moments with the stranger: the burning heart, the heartache, the heart wrenching.

Such was their elation that they could hardly finish the meal, and certainly not think of retiring for the night. Even in haste, the walk back to Jerusalem would take two hours or more, and it was now well after dark. Nevertheless, the two set out that instant, or at least "that same hour" (v. 33). The Eleven had already gathered with some others and had already come to believe that Jesus had, indeed, risen from the dead. They confirmed the story of Cleopas and his companion: Jesus had also appeared to Simon who could attest to it himself. In this mutual attestation we have one of the very earliest examples of the missionary dimension of Christianity: the community, convinced of the reality of the Risen Christ, is quite incapable of keeping the good news to itself.

The narrative ends with the two disciples telling their story, perhaps to inform the others about their extraordinary encounter, but surely also to hear themselves repeat the sequence of events and the gradual dawning of their Resurrection-consciousness. The story they told has been told again and again as a way of forming faith and firming faith. And it always ends at the table, with the breaking of the bread. That is where we recognize ourselves, our godliness, and our God.

But does it always end at the table, and should it end there? Sadly, there are times when we leave the table and never get back there to break and share the bread of our lives. And there are times when we do make it back to the table, but forget that we must then return to our Jerusalems and to the ends of the earth. For Luke, the storyteller, the table can only be a stage on the journey. There is a waiting world, deprived, even starved, and unsure of the meaning of its own life. And we are gathered in order to be scattered, called in order to be sent. When we become scattered we must gather again to remember; and when we have been sent we must invite others, in the name of the one who sends us, to believe that they too are called and sent.

The poignancy of the Emmaus account can serve as a great source of encouragement to all who are downhearted, discouraged, or depressed. There are certainly times when it is difficult to believe and to hope against hope. Even the encouragement, or testimony, of friends can sometimes fail to convince us. The purgative way is a lonely way, yet it is also a stretch of *the Way* of Jesus. Perhaps by sheer perseverance, simply by going through the motions of our lives (walking to Emmaus with a companion for reasons that are not even clear to us), we can remain in touch with life, and with others, in such a way that we do not become completely isolated and unreachable.

Jesus the stranger will seek us out and find us, if we are on the way, or seeking the way. He is *the Way*, and he will show us the meaning of our own existence if we acknowledge the foolishness, or mindlessness, that can mar and mark our lives. Jesus the stranger will interpret for us what may seem incomprehensible. Jesus the stranger will make our hearts burn again, as once they burned before. But Jesus the stranger comes to us as he always said he would: as a hungry man, a thirsty woman, a naked child, a sick grandmother, or a condemned prisoner. All we have to do is to be attentive, to visit the sick, to feed the hungry, to give drink to the thirsty, to clothe the naked, and to visit the imprisoned. Because so long as we are close to the very least— the nobodies of this world—then we are close to Jesus the stranger (Mt 25:35–40).

CHAPTER SEVENTEEN

Thomas Transformed

(Jn 20:24–29)

(24) *But Thomas (who was called the Twin), one of the twelve, was not with them when Jesus came.* (25) *So the other disciples told him, "We have seen the Lord." But he said to them, "Unless I see the mark of the nails in his hands, and put my finger in the mark of the nails and my hand in his side, I will not believe."*

(26) *A week later his disciples were again in the house, and Thomas was with them. Although the doors were shut, Jesus came and stood among them and said, "Peace be with you."* (27) *Then he said to Thomas, "Put your finger here and see my hands. Reach out your hand and put it in my side. Do not doubt but believe."* (28) *Thomas answered him, "My Lord and my God!"* (29) *Jesus said to him, "Have you believed because you have seen me? Blessed are those who have not seen and yet have come to believe."*

We come to the end of this series of encounters with Jesus, and there could be no more fitting conclusion than a reflection upon the appearance of Jesus to Thomas and on its implications not only for him but for ourselves.

"Doubting Thomas" is a phrase, and Thomas the Doubter is a personality, that has come into our language and culture. But in some ways it is unfortunate that many people who commonly use the phrase have absolutely no idea of its original context or, indeed, the ultimate outcome of the story from which Thomas earned his nickname.

According to John's Gospel, Jesus appeared to the Eleven on the evening of the day of Resurrection. If we are to square this account with that of Luke's Gospel (a risky venture, to be sure), we would surmise that after leaving the company of the companions at Emmaus, Jesus immediately returned to Jerusalem—as indeed also did the companions, though by some other means (Lk 24:31,33). The Risen Christ was not confined by space or time, and he appeared in a room with locked doors (Jn 20:19). We should not be surprised at this, but we do tend to be—perhaps because of our literalism and lack of imagination. For many Christians, and others too, the Resurrection is often thought of as a kind of resuscitation, whereby Jesus is reanimated by a reverse process that brings him back from death to life. That is simply because we cannot imagine what a resurrected body might be like: we have no precedent. But if we allow the Resurrection stories to be told, we might be able to allow ourselves to absorb them for what they tell us, rather than to remain unconvinced, due to the laws of physics they seem to contravene.

People of many cultures today would have absolutely no problem with the notion of bilocation or with the idea of a person passing through physical barriers such as walls. A person's spirit, being intrinsically freer that its embodied form, is understood not to be subject to the same constraints as the body. So Jesus, the ultimate victor over death, could be understood to be both in Emmaus and also entering a locked room some seven miles away. Likewise, a resurrected body would obey its own laws, laws unknown to those of us with mortal bodies. Thus, people of many cultures would simply accept what they cannot understand and turn to the lessons to be learned. We, however, tend not to accept what we cannot understand, so we often miss the lessons to be learned. It is both perverse and self-defeating. The legacy of the Enlightenment and Positivism is still very much among us.

We can approach the post-Resurrection stories in one of two ways. Either we can apply the laws of physics and logic as we know them in our scientific world, in which case we will find the stories to be literally incredible. Or we can approach these stories as disciples in search of faith, willing at least to suspend judgment, or better to listen to the stories and see what they are telling us. In the former case, we have simply nothing to learn. In the latter case, we may come to faith in Jesus without thereby presuming to understand what is simply above, or beyond, our understanding. The second approach seems to be worth the risk: when we cannot understand, it is sometimes wise to "stand under."

We are told, without elaboration, that Thomas was not with the surviving members of the Twelve when Jesus appeared to them on the evening of the day of his Resurrection. Where was he? We have no information; but the fact that the apostles seem to have been paralyzed into inaction, and to have clung together like limpets, may lead us to ask whether Thomas—who was absent—had already shown indications of being different during the previous months. The text we are exploring here, tells us, for the first time, that Thomas was called Didymus (which is translated as "twin"). Perhaps he had been holed up with his other twin, or with his family, on the first day of the week. Maybe that was why he was not with the rest of the apostles. Still, it is not easy to understand his motivation. But Thomas does seem to be a little different from the rest of the group, and we are bound to wonder how and why, given the story that will follow. Could there be any possible significance to the fact that the word *didymus* could also have the meaning of "testicles" and might be a reference to a nickname of some sort? Did he have an inferiority complex? Was he hiding from something? This is quite speculative, but intriguing, in view of what would happen next.

Didymus, then, was not present at the alleged appearance of Jesus, and he would not accept the testimony of those who were. This Thomas seems to be a rather volatile man: he does not simply refuse to believe, he makes a very extravagant and rather petulant, statement—more like an ultimatum—that is indirectly aimed at Jesus himself. Perhaps Thomas was simply hurting too much to be able to accept that Jesus had indeed returned in his absence. Perhaps he wanted Jesus to know just how empty and angry he was after the events of the previous Friday. His outburst certainly sounds like a cry for help, a *cri de coeur*.

In any event, he declares in no uncertain terms, the precise conditions under which he would be willing to believe what had been told to him. And the terms he sets are, effectively, impossible. Thomas seems to be drawing a line in the sand, saying that now, under absolutely no circumstances, will he ever believe Jesus, much less believe *in* Jesus. The stage is set for a dramatic encounter.

It is now a week later and again we have no information about what has transpired, about the activities, or indeed the newfound faith of those who witnessed the appearance of Jesus, or about the experiences of Thomas himself in the course of that week. But the Eleven are together, and the doors are shut—hardly a sign of open hospitality or readiness to spread the news of the Resurrection. As with the previous week (when it was clear that the disciples were hiding, and in fear of the Jews [v. 19]), Jesus suddenly made his appearance, and again repeated what he had previously said: "Peace be with you." He is bringing God's peace, *Shalom*. This is no cheap peace, no superficial feeling of well-being, but the peace that surpasses understanding and resides at the very deepest part of the human heart and spirit. Clearly, this shalom is badly, and urgently, needed. It is the peace that casts out fear and makes freedom and love possible again. It is the peace the world cannot give, already promised and offered by Jesus, first at the supper on the night before he died, and then again when he appeared to them the night he rose again. So, for the third time, Jesus offers peace and, perhaps its effects finally begin to break through into the fearful hearts of those he trusted most. But there is another matter to which he must attend.

Immediately after his peace offering, Jesus turns to Thomas, who must already have been caught in a maelstrom of emotions. Here is Jesus! Thomas can see this with his own eyes, though he can hardly believe them because they contradict what he knows about impenetrable closed doors and undoubtedly dead bodies. But Thomas knows that this is Jesus. And he remembers only too clearly his intemperate—and deeply disrespectful—challenge of the week before. Thomas must be completely humiliated and deeply shamed, caught as he is between the witnesses to his ultimatum and the person to whom it had been directed. But Jesus had just said "Peace," and Thomas must have felt the peace in that room, where all was suddenly still, and every eye was upon him.

This is the gentle Jesus, meek and mild. This is the Jesus who is always ready to forgive, to embrace, and to gather people to himself. And yet this is no simpering, spineless Jesus: he will gently lead Thomas, making him do, step by step, exactly what he had demanded that he be permitted to do. This is the longest moment of Thomas's life. It is an awesome, shocking, heart-stopping moment for Thomas. And it brings him, almost literally, to his knees.

Thomas had demanded to be allowed to put his finger in the nail marks and his hand into the gaping wound in Jesus' side. Deliberately, with eyes locked on Thomas, Jesus invited him to do exactly that. And as he did so Jesus gently invited him to doubt no longer but to believe. There is no indication that Thomas even raised his hand, and every indication that he did not raise his voice. In a whisper, full of both shame and faith, Thomas heard the words tumbling from his own lips: "My Lord and my God!" (v. 28). It may be the most succinct, the most complete, the most moving and the most faith-filled statement in the whole of the New Testament. There is no air left in Thomas's lungs, and there is no movement in the room.

And Jesus said to him, "Have you believed because you have seen me?" (v. 29). Yes indeed, Thomas had come to believe because he had seen with his own eyes what his mind could not possibly have allowed him to see. Yes, Thomas had come to faith the long way round, by the slow road. Yes, Thomas had finally come to faith, but by degrees, not like the woman with a hemorrhage or the man possessed, not like the bent-over woman or the well-woman. But like them all now, Thomas was *there*.

In that timeless moment, he must have understood what it all meant. In that lung-bursting instant, he must have remembered, and received the enlightenment of grace and the grace of enlightenment. Perhaps this is why Thomas has been such a favorite with so many down the years: we are like him; we come to faith by the long, slow route. But by the grace of God we do come eventually.

And Jesus concludes his gentle remonstrance and reminder, leaving us words to live by, and words to live up to, and words we cannot forget: "Blessed are those who have not seen and yet have come to believe" (v. 29).